Th

Mis*conception*

Files

By

Julia Stonehouse

Previously published under the title *Father's Seed, Mother's Sorrow: How the wrong 'facts of life' gave men control of the world*.

Published by Julia Stonehouse, author of *Idols to Incubators: Reproduction theory through the ages*, Scarlet Press, London, 1994.

Copyright © Julia Stonehouse 2017

The author asserts her moral right to be identified as the author of this work.

All rights reserved. No part of this work, whether written or illustrative, may be reproduced or transmitted in any form or by any means, electronic or mechanical, including by any information storage or retrieval system, photocopy or recording, without prior permission in writing from the author.

Quotes from other authors within this work are similarly subject to copyright law and cannot be re-quoted or their words reproduced, transmitted or stored in any form whatsoever without first obtaining permission from that author or the publisher of that work.

Front and back cover illustrations by Nikolai Kozin.

ISBN-13: 978-1545438824
ISBN-10: 154543882X

www.themisconceptionfiles.com

Preface

The biggest mistake of our collective lives was to misunderstand where human life came from. Until the turn of the 20th century people had no idea about the true facts of life. Instead, they had one misconception after another – seriously flawed notions that deeply affected how they perceived themselves and organised their societies. Before 1900 the most widespread misconception was that there was just one seed of life, which came from the male and was planted in the womb of the female. This idea robbed women of everything including their children, their land, and their dignity. And because this male-seed misconception is still prevalent in many areas of the world today, we see cultural clashes relating to the position of women.

It was extremely difficult to discover the facts of life. Everything happens inside the body, away from view. It took generations of embryologists over 100 years to reach the conclusion that there are two seeds and fusion. This was a revelation because up to this point we understood life to emanate from one seed, as it does with plants: you put one seed in the ground and an entire plant grows from it, laden with fruit and the seed of future generations. One seed. That fact misled us for millennia.

I believe it is impossible to understand any feminist issue without first understanding a particular society's misconceptions because they led directly to attitudes, traditions, social structures, and institutions. But we have overlooked mis*conception* as a subject and consequently do not understand how we got where we are. And without recognising the impact of false 'facts of life,' we're destined to misunderstand not only our own history but that of our neighbours in the global village. Also, we project our own experience back in time and assume patriarchy has always been a 'natural' feature of male-female relationships. It has not. Before the male-seed theory of life there were other ideas about where life came from and we can see that, before his-story, there was her-story.

CONTENTS

Introduction

PART ONE: FATHER'S SEED, MOTHER'S SORROW　　　　　　Page 4

1: Father's Seed
2: Mother's Sorrow
3: The Ram, Lamb, Chicken and Egg
4: The Respected Men of Science
5: All Women Childless
6: Inheritance
7: Chastity
8: Gender Polarity: Confirmed by Science
9: Religion
10: So Why Has There Never Been A Female Bach or Beethoven?
11: Non-People
12: Conjugal Rights, Rape, Child Abuse
13: A Resemblance to Mother
14: Women Liberated From Incubator Status
15: My Hero
16: The Failed Ovum Seekers
17: The Man with the Peas
18: Sperm – The Little Animalcules
19: Let's Do What They Did
20: Other Theories of Reproduction
21: The Cover-up
22: Does it Matter?
23: Patriarchy Understood

PART TWO: THE WIDER HORIZON　　　　　　Page 79

24: The Wider Horizon
25: Islands in the Sun
26: Deep in the Forest
27: An Alternative Life-View
28: Woman the Hunter
29: Woman the Provider
30: Control Freaks
31: Monkey Talk
32: The Dental Records
33: Women: The Civilizing Force

PART THREE: HER STORY   Page 105

    34: Her Story
    35: Uncovering the Ancient Past
    36: Women who Reproduce on their Own
    37: Messages from the Big Freeze: 35,000-10,000 BC
    38: Images of the Ice Age Female: Sex Object? Fertility Charm? Creatrix?
    39: The Power of Blood: Life and Death
    40: Hunting Magic
    41: The First Revolution
    42: Woman's Perennial Seed
    43: Man the Waterer
    44: The Egg
    45: Animal Husbandry
    46: They Made Love, Not War
    47: The Blood-Line
    48: The Evolution of Gods
    49: Liberated Women
    50: Patterns of Female Power
    51: The Power behind the Throne
    52: Sexual Freedom
    53: The Sacrificial King
    54: Woman the Inventor
    55: Who was the Goddess?
    56: The History of the Phallus

PART FOUR: THE TAKE-OVER   Page 198

    57: The Take-Over
    58: Native Americans: A Take-Over and Cover-Up
    59: Yahweh: Another Take-Over
    60: Adam and Eve
    61: Living a Double Life

PART FIVE   Page 220

    62: "I Thought People Have Always Known the Facts of Life"

INTRODUCTION

Patriarchy was inevitable because people had the facts of life wrong. Until the turn of the 20th century, scientists and most other people thought there was a singular source of human seed that came from the testicles of the father and was put in the 'soil' of the woman. Women were not thought to be 'mothers' in the way we understand the word. Obviously women grew the children within, and gave birth, but they were not the source of seed so not parents as such. Men were the source of the seed, and that made the grown seed, the children, theirs.

This male-seed idea led directly to other ideas. First, there seemed to be a profound 'natural' distinction between the seed, men, and the soil, women. Because women had no seed, they had no reproductive rights. They did not reproduce. At the same time their bodies were clearly designed to grow and give birth to babies. This gave rise to the notion that women were men's baby-making machines and that men had the right to control the means of their own reproduction. Indeed, they had to control women because if she had a baby it would either be 100% his child, or 100% some other man's.

The male-seed version of 'nature' led to the idea that men were closer to God. While God created everything, men created something. Women, on the other hand, created nothing. They provided the environment in which the child could grow, and the material that fed the child. But women were not the source of the creative seed, merely its temporary resting place. They were just tools for men's creative spark.

Girls were an evolutionary dead-end. To continue his male ancestral seed-line, a man had to have a son. Inheritance of land went the same way as biological inheritance – through the male line. Why leave your land to a daughter when she will marry a man from another family and have children who belong, not to her, but to her husband? Why work hard all your life only to leave everything to another man's family?

The male-seed idea of reproduction had many ramifications and was the mortar that gave strength and permanence to the towers of patriarchy. When the patriarchal system is viewed through the perspective of the male-seed idea, it all begins to make sense. This is why reproduction theory is liberating. It becomes easy to understand not only why patriarchy happened, but that it was logical. At least, it was logical to people who had an incorrect idea about the 'facts of life'.

Patriarchal traditions are lingering, long after the cause of patriarchy has gone. This is because the roots of patriarchy are not understood. Most people I meet think "people have always known the facts of life." Nothing could be further from the truth. The discovery that woman also contributed 'seed', in the form of the ovum, was absorbed into the literature without reference to the fact its existence had been denied for millennia. Men did not like the idea that the privileges they had enjoyed for so long were based on a big mistake. The cover-up was so effective, the embryologists who worked hard to unravel the mystery of life were quietly airbrushed out of history. They were the heroes of women's liberation from incubator status but their names are not generally known.

Archaeologists often say "men discovered their role in reproduction around 10,000 BC." That is wrong by 12,000 years because men's role was only "discovered" in 1900 AD. But certainly there was a change in thinking around 10,000 BC, which can be seen in the iconography of the time.

In Part Three of this book I go back into prehistory and try to figure out what people thought about reproduction. There seem to be two distinct periods of time. During 10-3,000 BC it appears that many people thought the seed was in the woman, and needed 'water' from a man to make it germinate and grow. As the source of the seed, the woman was thought to be the parent, while the man was just her reproductive helper. That's why there were so many goddess religions at that time. Before

10,000 BC, all the evidence points to people thinking women reproduced on their own, without men. That may seem a bizarre concept but it was actually quite a widespread idea in some parts of the world, even up to recent times, and certain small groups of people still believe it today.

Reproduction theory is a key feminist issue, but it has been overlooked in the literature – probably because of the widespread notion that "people have always known the facts of life." The revolution that occurred around the turn of the 20th century, which credited women with actual parenthood, was a silent event.

Reproduction theory does not happen in a bubble. It seeps like a fog into every crevice of life. It affects religion, philosophy, and law. It has its own history, and prehistory. We are talking embryology, biology, psychology, anthropology and archaeology. This is a very wide-ranging subject.

Reproduction theory is very relevant today because there are people in the world living with the new biology (two seeds and fusion), while others are still living with the traditions engendered by the old biology (male seed/female soil). There is a huge chasm of misunderstanding between us. At the same time, we're entering a new world of reproduction in which people are playing God with DNA they can buy on the internet. It is now crucial that we understand the role reproduction theory has had on the world, so we can move forward better prepared.

PART ONE: FATHER'S SEED, MOTHER'S SORROW

1: FATHER'S SEED

Seeds are singular. They embody the power of one. Take one seed, put it in the ground, wait, and watch a plant grow from it, laden with more seeds. Each tiny pip in an apple can produce an entire tree, laden with more apples, and many more pips. One little acorn can produce an oak tree, bursting with more acorns. Over time, one pip has the potential to create a fruit-filled orchard, and one acorn can generate an entire lush forest.

When people began to wonder where the human seed came from they thought in terms of a singular seed. They didn't know there are two seeds - ovum and sperm - and fusion. How would they know that? They couldn't even imagine it. You don't see farmers squish two seeds together and then put them in the ground. In the debate about human reproduction, it was a question of either/or: "does the seed come from the mother?" or "does the seed come from the father?"

We have evidence - from the ancient Greeks right up to the turn of the 20th century - that people over much of the world thought there was one seed of human life, and it came from the male. This is the basic theory: the seed comes from the father's testicles and he plants it in the furrow of the female vulva, and deep within her soil. The menstrual blood, which stops when the seed has 'taken', goes to make the body of the child. The woman obviously plays a crucial role in the development of the child but, when that child emerges from her body, it will be father's grown seed. The temporary growing place, the mother, the earth, will have no rights over it.

Anthropologist Leela Dube researched the male seed/female soil concept in India in the 1980's and found it to be very widely held:

"In his body man has the seed: the woman, on the other hand, is herself the field ... Her whole body is conceived of as contributing towards the growth of the foetus, while the breasts are getting ready for providing nourishment after the child leaves the womb. The two partners are not at par with one another in so far as the process of reproduction is concerned. The offspring belongs to one to whom the seed belongs. In fact, he also owns the field. Both the seed and the field belong to man."

But the problem with the male seed/female soil theory is that it leads to a whole set of other thoughts that had, and continue to have, a very negative impact on women, as Dube explains:

"...the supposed unequal contribution of the two sexes to human reproduction as expressed through the symbolism of 'seed and earth' provides the rationalization for a system in which woman stands alienated from productive resources, has no control over her own labour power, and is denied rights over her own offspring."

Working in the 1980's in Eastern Turkey, anthropologist Carol Delaney found the same male-seed culture. The language is very revealing. The words for 'to be pregnant', *gebe kalmak*, translate as 'the seed remained and will swell up'. The male seed is referred to as *canh*, as 'having soul or life in it'. The male role is 'to put the seed in' (*dollemek*) the vagina - *dolyolu*, which translates literally as 'seedpath', which leads to 'the seedbed' (*dolyatagt*). Delaney found that men and women's contribution is thought of as being completely different:

Men's Contribution	Women's Contribution
"With seed, men appear to provide the creative spark of life, the essential identity of the child; ..."	"... while women, like soil, contribute the nurturant material that sustains it..."

"The perceived creative, life-giving ability of men allies them symbolically with God …"	" … whereas the material sustenance provided by women associates them with what was created by God, namely the earth."
"semen or seed is a finer concoction of blood, and semen is the medium through which the divine, eternal element (soul) is transmitted"	"women's blood seems to be something additive, thought of more as food"

The father's side of the family is known as the *sulb tarafi*, *sulb* meaning loins, descendants and seed; while the mother's side of the family is known as the *sut tarafi*, the milk side. Only a man has an *aile*, a family; while a woman is just part of one – her father's, husband's, brother's, or son's. A man is the seed that goes on and on; only he produces *filiz*, shoots or buds (children), which give him continuity into the future. But a woman is reproductively transient – she does a job, then dies, leaving no human legacy. In the male-seed scenario, all females are evolutionary dead-ends.

This male-seed theory continues to have a strong hold on cultures all over the world and was the prevailing theory in Europe when 19th century scientists set out to establish the exact mechanism of creating life. But, because everything happens inside the woman's body, the facts were extremely difficult to establish. It took decades for them to realise that every venerated man of science since the ancient Greeks had got the facts of life wrong. Then the scientists realised another problem: because the male-seed theory had become enshrined in religion, to challenge it was blasphemous. Also, a quagmire of traditions had built up around the male-seed theory, and that made presenting an alternative life-view extremely hard work.

It did not help that the experimental research was being

carried out on newts, frogs, sea urchins, fruit flies and garden peas. Although the scientists could extrapolate from this work and hypothesise that human reproduction was essentially the same as newts, even in 1900 AD there were plenty of people, especially in religious circles, who refused to believe we had anything in common with this lowly form of pond life. The argument could only come to a final halt when photographic proof was produced showing human sperm entering human ovum. The year was 1960.

If you ask the question "When did people discover the facts of human life?" the latest date would be when we got physical proof in 1960, and the earliest date would be 1827, when the mammalian ovum was discovered by Karl Ernst von Baer. But, as we shall see, nobody took notice of von Baer and even he was very reluctant to draw any conclusions from what he found. So it would still require a long slog in embryological research until 1900 when science felt confident enough to form a consensus view of human reproduction – still a hypothesis though: there is ovum and sperm fusion.

These are surprisingly late dates. Before I started researching this subject, like most people I thought "people have always known the facts of life." But nothing could be further from the truth. Finding out the facts of life was one of the hardest scientific battles of all time and the strange thing is very few people know anything about it. I can say that because I've been lecturing on the subject for years and have yet to meet anyone who has heard of Karl Ernst von Baer or Herman Fol – two of the many embryologists whose combined work over many decades liberated woman from incubator status.

The entire scientific subject has been swept under the carpet. The question is "why?" Maybe it's as simple as the truism "the nature of power is to retain your power," because the notion that men were the source of human seed gave them supreme power, and an inflated sense of their own superiority, and at the time of the 'disappearance' they were still in charge.

SELECTED REFERENCES:
Dube, Leela, 'Seed and Earth: The Symbolism of Biological Reproduction and Sexual Relations of Production' in *Visibility and Power*, Eds.: Dube, Leacock, Ardener, Delhi: Oxford University Press, 1986, pages 41 and 44.
Delaney, Carol, *The Seed and the Soil: Gender and Cosmology in Turkish Village Society*, pages 8 and 154, © 1994 by the Regents of the University of California. Published by the University of California Press.

2: MOTHER'S SORROW

Imagine two bodies lying on the floor in front of you – one is dead, and the other is alive but very still, eyes blinking. In the male-seed way of thinking, both got their body from the woman who gave birth to them. She provided the physical material they're made of, the blood and flesh. The one who is alive, however, is alive only because they still have the spark of life they got from their father. That 'alive-ness' was carried in the male seed and gave the body its ability to move about. This meant that men were responsible for the difference between life and death. It was also said that men's seed provided the blueprint for the body, and the 'sentient soul' – the thinking, creative part – that which makes us human.

In the male-seed life-view, women provide a place for the seed to grow. She's like the oven you cook buns in. But the buns, like the crop from the earth, belong to the baker, or the farmer. They are not the woman's buns.

Until the 20th century, a woman wasn't a 'mother' in the way we understand it. She was a temporary necessity in the process of gestation, certainly, and she fed the babies from her breast and cared for them. But she had no rights over them. She did not have children; she incubated men's children. And there's the crucial difference.

Now we think children are only 50% men's and we have the equation to prove it – 23 chromosomes from the father and 23 from the mother, making the 46 each human develops from.

But imagine being a woman in the male-seed era: you have no chromosomes to contribute, no genetic material at all, no DNA, no ovum, no seed, no nothing. You're an empty shell – infertile. And that is how all women felt during the male-seed era, and how millions of women around the world are still made to feel today in many cultures around the world.

With the male-seed way of thinking, certain other thoughts follow as inevitably as night follows day. We'll go through these later, but the first obvious thought is that a man has to have sons. Without sons, there is no continuation of the male seed that came from grandpa, and great-grandpa and so forth back to the beginning of time. Without sons, your family line has come to a grinding halt. Daughters are no consolation because they're an evolutionary dead-end. They do not carry seed within them so they don't continue anything. If you're going to choose between having a son and a daughter, you have to choose a son. And, because male-seed thinking is still going on, this is precisely the choice being made in many parts of the world today.

When people talk about 'infanticide' they're really talking about female infanticide. Usually for reasons of poverty, millions of infant girls have been, and continue to be, killed around the world. And because we now have sex-detection ultrasound technology, the problem is getting worse. According to a 2008 joint report by UK charity ActionAid and the Canadian government's International Development Research Centre, there are only 706 baby girls to every 1,000 baby boys in urban areas of the Indian state of Punjab. The report estimates that, over the last twenty years, ten million female foetuses have been aborted in India. And the UK medical journal, *The Lancet*, likewise calculates that half a million female foetuses are being aborted every year. At over 13,000 a day, female infanticide is now big business – even though it's illegal.

People who can't afford the scan and abortion revert to traditional means of killing baby girls when they're born. The report mentioned above highlights a common method being used in India – allow the umbilical cord to become infected. Smothering and drowning are also old favourites. One Pakistani friend told me that in his village they disposed of unwanted baby girls by rolling them down a hill. If they lived, it was God's will. Most, of course, died. In China, which had a 'one-child' policy of family planning for 30 years until 2015, 12% of girls are 'missing', which means dead. There are now 40 million extra men in the population, unable to find a woman to marry. This disparity in gender is despite government policy to outlaw the use of scans for sex identification of the foetus, and is caused by the intense impetus to produce a seed-carrying son. Even when people know that females also carry seed, strongly-held traditional values over-ride any modern and logical reasoning.

Many traditions were inevitable consequences of the male-seed idea. For example, in many poor countries parents want sons to act as guardians and providers in their old age. Daughters are no good because they will marry into another family, move away, and have children that belong to the husband's family. Parents will be abandoned by daughters, but looked after by sons. Moreover, this lessening of female value has led to the parents having to provide a dowry – they give her away, and pay the groom's family for taking her off their hands. Clearly, parents with two daughters who need a dowry to get married are going to struggle financially, or even be ruined financially, whereas parents with two sons can look forward to a comfortable and secure old age. In many cultures, too, only a son can carry out the parent's funeral rites, and only a son can continue with his seed the family line that originated with the male ancestors, who need to be honoured. Bringing the venerated male ancestral line to a grinding halt by only having a female child brings humiliation and shame on her parents.

Royal families throughout history have been obsessed with the production of male heirs. In the 16th century, when Catherine of Aragon failed to produce a son for King Henry VIII of England, Henry sought permission from the Catholic Pope in Rome to divorce her. The Pope refused so, in 1534, Henry changed the religion of the country from Catholic to Protestant, so he could marry his mistress, Ann Boleyn. This flung the country into a religious war that lasted 100 years. Japan has been in a state of constitutional panic over the fact that for over 40 years no male heir had been born within the Japanese royal family. A huge collective sigh of relief could be heard in 2006 when Prince Hisahito was born, becoming next in line to the throne in preference not only to his two older sisters, but to his female cousin who is the child of the current Crown Prince. The United Kingdom only came to its constitutional senses in 2015, when the law was changed to allow gender equality in terms of succession and inheritance in the royal family.

SELECTED REFERENCES:
Report by Action Aid and International Development Research Centre, Canada, 2008, pages 3, 4 and 18:
http://www.actionaid.org.uk/doc_lib/disappearing_daughters_0608.pdf

3: THE RAM, LAMB, CHICKEN AND EGG

If you wanted to prove that the female was as important in reproduction as the male, everything in nature was against you. First, everyone knew that with no ram, there was no lamb. If you have a field full of female sheep, or nanny goats, or cows, they'll not produce offspring unless there's a male to mount them. We know that the male semen fuses with female ovum – but only because we've had the benefit of science to tell us. Without that knowledge, people thought the male delivered seed into the 'soil' of the female animal.

Second, they knew that if a chicken produced an egg without having been mounted by a rooster, that egg decomposes. On the other hand, when a chicken lays an egg after being mounted by a rooster, that egg will crack open and reveal a live chick. To a people used to thinking in terms of a single seed, the male rooster provided that seed.

The third way people discussed this subject was in terms of "milk and rennet." Rennet is curdled milk that transforms liquid milk into cheese. The milk was equated with female menstrual blood, and rennet with semen. Without rennet, the milk goes sour; with rennet, it transforms into cheese. Aristotle, the ancient Greek whose ideas were influential for two thousand years, said the "vital heat" of semen, turned menstrual blood into a child.

Over the millennia, and still in many countries around the world, people referred to all the above analogies to explain why the male contribution to human reproduction was the active, and superior, principle. Soil without seed is just a clod of earth. A sheep without semen from a ram has no lambs. A chicken without a rooster lays eggs that decompose. And milk without rennet is just rancid.

Whichever theory people used, it was evidence that the male, "active principle," was the source of the seed and the spark of life, while the female contribution was non-generative *stuff* the active male principle worked its magic on. It was an either-or world these people were, and are, living in, and it leads directly to a very polarised view of the 'nature' of men, and of women.

4: THE RESPECTED MEN OF SCIENCE

Over the centuries, there were famous male philosophers and men of science who used the word "seed" to describe what the woman contributed to human reproduction, but this word was only used to describe physical matter from the woman – such as her menstrual blood or her sexual secretions. They did not mean the words "female seed" in the way we would understand it. To them, and all the people around them, it was taken as a known given fact that women contribute no reproductive material. Here are some examples of what was said:

Who said it?	Of Men:	Of Women:
Aeschylus (through Apollo in *Eumenides*) Greek playwright 458 BC	"The thruster, the father, is the true parent …"	"The mother is not the true source of life; We call her mother but she is more the nurse; The furrow where the seed is thrust … The woman but tends the growing plant; With God's grace, the host that shelters the stranger-guest."
Aristotle Greek scholar 350 BC	"the male semen cooks and shapes menstrual blood into a new human being"	Menstruation "is analogous in females to the semen in males"
Aristotle 350 BC	Males provide the "sentient soul"	Females provide the "prime matter"; it is "plain that the female does not contribute semen to the generation of offspring"
Aristotle 350 BC	"The male stands for the effective and the active, …"	"…and the female … for the passive"
Aristotle 350 BC	"that which comes into being is male, is better and more divine …"	"… than the material whereby it is female"
Aristotle 350 BC	Men are the carpenters, who with their creative force, give shape and form to the object (the baby).	Women are the wood (matter/stuff), used by the carpenters to make a new object (the baby).

Aristotle 350 BC	"The male provides the 'form' and the 'principle of the movement'"; "Of course the active elements are always higher on any scale, and more divine."	The woman provides the material.
Galen *Greek anatomist* *129-199 AD*		Referring to liquid produced by a woman during sexual excitement, which he called 'seed': (it) "contributes nothing to the generation of offspring." It gives pleasure, provides lubrication, and nourishment.
Galen *129-199 AD*	Men have the optimum amount of heat.	The vagina is an imperfect, under-developed penis, that it was "formed within her when she was still a foetus, but could not because of the defect in the heat emerge and project on the outside."
Ibn Sina (Avicenna) *Iranian philosopher and physician* *980-1037*	"… the seed of man is the principle of movement."	"Clearly the seed of woman is fit to be matter, but not fit to be the principle of movement …"

Ibn Sina (Avicenna) 980-1037	(The male semen) "… is in every organ like the moving principle. From it the soul is formed"	
Ricardo Anglici Anatomist, 12th century	(Semen) provides the "spirit and creative power and form."	
Albertus Magnus 'Doctor Universalis' German Theologian/ Patron Saint of Natural Sciences c.1200-1280	The male seed gives form.	Menstrual fluid provides the "matter" of the baby. The role of female sexual secretions are: "preparing and enabling matter to receive the action from the operator, that is, man's sperm."
Thomas Aquinas Italian Theologian/ Philosopher 1225-1274	Men's "active seminal power gives form to …"	"… the corporeal matter, which is supplied by the mother." (Note: 'corporeal' means physical, bodily, mortal, of the nature of the animal body as opposed to the spirit)
Antoni van Leeuwenhoek Discovered sperm in 1675, Dutch 1632-1723	Sperm are an early stage of the foetus - in the same way that an insect larva is an earlier stage of the insect it becomes; or an apple seed is the source of an apple tree.	The Graafian follicle is non-generative; it is a warm nest with built-in storehouse – a nutritive womb within the womb. The "yolk" gives the

		sperm "the first nourishment."
Richard Bradley *Chair of Biology, Cambridge University* *1688-1732* Quote 1721	"seminal animalcules" (sperm) are the "principles of generation or the beginning of man and other animals"	
Jean Astruc *French professor of medicine* *1684-1766* Quote 1740	The "vermiculus" (sperm) produces the foetus – which belongs to the father.	Woman has an "egg" which feeds the sperm and becomes the placenta and membranous sack around the foetus.
Comte de Buffon *French naturalist* *1707-1788* Quote 1785	"the male semen is the sculptor …"	"… the menstrual blood is the block of marble, and the foetus is the figure which is fashioned out of this combination."
Erasmus Darwin *English physician and naturalist* *1731-1802* Quote 1794	"…the embryo is provided by the male …"	" … and the oxygen, food and nidus by the female"

This last quote is from the grandfather of Charles Darwin. We think of Charles as a radical forward thinker, and he was as far as evolution theory was concerned. But, like everyone else around at the time, he knew very little about reproduction. In 1868 he outlined a theory called "pangenesis," and suggested that "gemmules" travelled around in the bloodstream gathering up traits that would be inherited, like long eyelashes or an ear for music.

We can forgive a bizarre theory like this because finding out the facts of life was extremely difficult and took hundreds of scientists centuries to achieve. What is less forgivable, however, is that respected men in positions of influence also lied to keep the male-seed theory going. The man credited with being "the founder of experimental physiology" was Galen of Pergamon, a Greek living in the Roman Empire in the 2nd century AD who became physician to Roman emperors. He's important to the story because his ideas about reproduction were taken seriously for 1,750 years. But Galen was a sexist, living in a sexist age. It was also an age with a lot of silly notions floating about. One of these was that females were created by the left side of the body, and males by the right. To prove the inferiority of the left side, Galen described the abdominal veins incorrectly so the left-side organs were fed by blood that had not been cleansed by the kidneys. He wrote "the left testes in the male and the left uterus in the female receive blood still un-cleansed, full of residues, watery and serous." Meanwhile, he described the right-sided abdominal veins correctly, with the blood cleansed by the kidneys, to distinguish the purer, male side.

At this time people thought that impurity generates less heat. So, according to Galen, because the left (female) side is fed with un-cleansed and impure blood, which has less heat, seed produced on the left is not cooked to perfection like that on the right, which can and does produce the perfect, i.e. male, seed.

Galen thought the vagina was an under-developed penis that could not, because of this female lack of heat, "emerge and project on the outside." So although Galen does use the word female "seed," he lied to prove women only produced inferior, sterile, non-generative "seed" and were, moreover, under-developed men.

It's unlikely Galen ever dissected a human body and as the Christian Church banned human dissection, Galen's lies could not be disproved and his left-sided impure/under-developed/uncooked and imperfect female "seed" notion continued to be accepted for centuries. Even when the great anatomist Andreas Vesalius gained access to the executed bodies of criminals and published his findings in 1543, he did not correct Galen's error with the veins, even though he did correct many other, less contentious, details of Galen's anatomy. And so the notion of female "seed" being impure and non-generative continued for another few hundred years.

These men are supposed to be heroes of science history but in truth they were just heroes for sexist men because they contributed to the great cover-up that has left us even today with a social and institutional legacy that was a consequence of male-seed superiority. There was never any hope for women to be considered equal to men while the ideas of Aristotle and Galen permeated Western and Middle Eastern cultures. In the case of Aristotle, his sexist ideas were influential for 2,250 years. Galen noted that "Aristotle was right in thinking the female less perfect than the male" and 500 years after Aristotle added his own opinion, "within mankind the man is more perfect than the woman."

The inferiority of women was grounded in theories of reproduction that we can see today were utterly ridiculous, nevertheless throughout the historical period generations of men of science repeated them, and extrapolated from them to come to erroneous conclusions about the 'nature' of women. They each had their own sexist spin on the issue, drawing all manner of analogies to emphasise the superiority of the male. One of my favourites is Galen: "just as the mole has imperfect eyes ... so too the woman is less perfect than the man in respect of the generative parts." Women were half-blind pathetic creatures living underground while men strode the earth – a scenario justified by incorrect reproduction theory.

SELECTED REFERENCES:
Tuana, Nancy, 'The Sexist Bias of Reproductive Theory', in N. Tuana (Ed.),

Feminism and Science, Bloomington: Indiana University Press, 1989, page 156.

5: ALL WOMEN CHILDLESS

We're so used to thinking of 'women and children' as an inextricably linked unit, it's very hard to conceptualise the reality of the male-seed past and present in which children are not 50% hers, as we experience it, but 0% hers. This is how the seed travels down the male line:

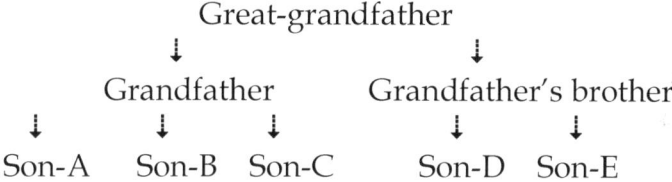

All the sons, A-C and D-E, get their seed from the same great-grandfather. So if a woman has a child by Son-A, the child's family is not her, or her parents or siblings because she contributed no seed. The child's relatives are their father, his father, and grandfather, and sons B and C. The next closest family is grandfather's brother and his sons, D and E.

What this means in the real world is that if she wants to divorce, she may never see the children again. I'm sure we've all seen on TV or read in the press stories about Western women who married a man from another culture who, when they divorced, abducted the children and took them back to his home country. We find it terrible and have complete sympathy for the woman. It only seems natural to us that children belong with their mothers. But many cultures around the world are still living with the tradition of male-seed reproduction and as far as they're concerned, the child rightfully belongs with the father's family. For example, Leela Dube writes of India:

"... in situations of conflict the language of seed and field is used to assert the paternal right. After a domestic quarrel if the wife threatens to leave the husband, the latter would promptly say 'you may go if you want, but leave my seedling with me'."

In all male-seed cultures, fathers will particularly want to keep the boys. Although the mother may be allowed to bring him up until a certain age, after puberty he will return to the father's home. As girls have none of father's seed, they're often allowed to stay with the mother.

If the father dies, the woman won't be able to go somewhere else and make a new life for herself and the children, because the children will now be under the control of father's nearest male relative. If that relative is nice, he may allow the woman to live with his family so she can look after his family seed – i.e. the children that grew in her womb. But if he's nasty, he'll tell her to pack her bags and leave the children with him. And many legal systems around the world will support him in that decision.

This seems very harsh to us, but it's completely understandable to people who have traditionally thought in terms of male-seed reproduction. In Eastern Turkey, anthropologist Carol Delaney found a society "that imagines men as 'creators' and 'owners' of children, who partake of their essence and are indeed part of themselves." When explaining why children belonged to the father in the case of divorce, villages said men were *cocok sahibi*, literally, child-owners.

In Arabic countries people have long names that express their paternal lineage. For example, the name Sa'id ibn Kasim ibn Ali ibn Husayn explains that this man, Sa'id, is the son of Kasim, the son of Ali, the son of Husayn. Likewise, his sister, Fatima, would be Fatima bint Kasim bint Ali bint Husayn. In Western culture, likewise, children traditionally adopt their father's name, and when a woman is 'given away' by her father at marriage, she drops the 'family name' - father's name – and is given the name of another man, her husband. These may just be traditions we go along with without much thought, but they're rooted in a time when women in our culture had few rights, either over their own destiny, or that of the children.

We live in a very dynamic world with people moving from country to country, and marrying outside their own nationality, so looking at how laws of citizenship apply to children is one way to see how particular cultures trace family lines. For example, a child born to an Iranian father – no matter where that child is born – is considered an Iranian citizen. A child born to a married couple from Indonesia can become a citizen if the father is Indonesian. In Malaysia, a child's racial group is taken to be their father's ethnic group, whatever the ethnicity of the mother.

Many countries are in transition from patrilineal laws that only give citizenship through the father, to laws that also give citizenship to the child if the mother is from the country. For example, in India, citizenship could only be conferred through the father until 1992, when descent through the mother was also allowed. In Japan, citizenship was only through the father until 1984. And in both the UK and Italy citizenship was only through the father until 1948.

The laws regarding the custody of children are also revealing. In the UK, women had no legal rights over children before 1878. Over the next hundred years there were many small changes in the law until, finally, in 1973, The Guardianship Act stated: "a mother shall have the same rights and authority as the law allows to a father, and the rights and authority of mother and father shall be equal and be exercisable by either without the other." When these words were being enshrined in law, Pink Floyd had the top selling UK album with 'Dark Side of the Moon' … and it wasn't that long ago.

Today in England and Wales there's a campaign to have the name of the bride and groom's mothers added to a marriage certificate. As of writing this in 2017, only fathers' names appear on this important legal documentation. This inequality is a direct legacy of the notion that a child is the grown seed of the father. It takes a very long time for things to change.

SELECTED REFERENCES:
Dube, Leela, 'Seed and Earth: 'The Symbolism of Biological Reproduction and Sexual Relations of Production' in *Visibility and Power*, Eds.: Dube, Leacock, Ardener, Delhi: Oxford University Press, 1986, page 29.
Delaney, Carol, *The Seed and the Soil: Gender and Cosmology in Turkish Village Society*, page 167, © 1994 by the Regents of the University of California. Published by the University of California Press.

6: INHERITANCE

The inheritance of land and wealth went the same way as biological inheritance – through the male. It would be stupid to leave your land to a daughter. She'll marry a man from another family, and have children – who will be the grown seed of her husband. Why would you work hard all your life only to give it to another man's family?

In 1776, the writer James Boswell pondered the question of whether to leave his estate to heirs of both sexes, or to male heirs only:

"I...had a zealous partiality for heirs male, however remote, which I maintained by arguments which appeared to me to have considerable weight - As first, the opinion of some distinguished naturalists, that our species is transmitted through males only, the female being all along no more than a nidus, or nurse, as Mother Earth is to plants of every sort; which notion seems to be confirmed by that text of Scripture, 'He was yet in the loins of his father when Melchisedec met him' (Heb. vii, 10), and consequently, that a man's grandson by a daughter ... has, in reality, no connection whatever with his blood."

At this time most men didn't think about inheritance and left their land and most of their wealth and possessions to sons or, if they didn't have them, "heirs male, however remote." As we have seen, remote male heirs can all trace their biological inheritance backward in time, along the male line, to the same grandfather, or great-grandfather ... the source of all the family seed. Give a daughter a dowry, enough the help her through life, but it doesn't make sense to worry about the next generation because her children aren't 'family'.

In many places and times it was against the law to leave land to a daughter. Salic law was codified in France in the early 6th century and became the basis for the laws of many European countries. It states "no portion of the inheritance shall come to a woman: but the whole inheritance of the land shall come to the male sex." In cases where there were no male family members, a daughter could inherit after an amendment made in 570 AD, with the idea that she would hold it until she had sons, who would then inherit. The Christian churches have their own Canon Law, which has been influential since Saxon times in the UK. For hundreds of years it didn't allow girls or women to inherit property, preferring it to go to males or, as it was called, "the worthiest of blood."

The upshot of all this is that today, according to the charity Oxfam, women only own 1% of the property in the world, although they do 66% of the work and provide 50% of the food. And while men earn 90% of the income, women only earn 10%.

SELECTED REFERENCES:
Boswell, James, *The Life of Dr. Johnson*, various editions, letter and note January 1776.

7: CHASTITY

When a woman has a baby she knows it's hers – she can feel it, and see it, emerging from between her legs. Men have no such certainty. This is worrying enough for them when they think the baby is (or isn't) 50% theirs, but when they think the baby is either 100% theirs, or 100% some other man's, it's a whole other ball game.

Men have no control over the reproductive process because they don't have a womb. But, when they're living with the male-seed life-view, women's bodies appear expressly designed to carry male seed to fruition. And as women have no seed, they don't reproduce themselves, which means they don't deserve or warrant having reproductive rights. This, then, was the stark difference that led men to feel they had to control their baby-making machines absolutely.

In the male-seed life-view, female chastity becomes men's number one priority. And she not only has to be chaste, but seen to be chaste. This means women can't be out of sight of their family, wander around on their own, dress provocatively, hang around in male company, or generally give the impression they're sexually available. In many parts of the world there is even little sympathy for the woman who has been raped. This thinking has a very long tradition. In the book of Deuteronomy (22: 28-9) in the Old Testament of the Bible, a law is decreed saying that if a virgin is raped she must marry the rapist. It's written as a punishment for the man, who must pay the girl's father 50 shekels and is not allowed to later divorce her, without any apparent concern for the fate of the poor girl who must now be wed for life to her rapist.

The 'purity' of the female womb has long been the primary, male, concern and in more ignorant times a man had no way of knowing how 'soiled' a woman became after having sex with another man. Even if the woman had been raped, there was little sympathy for her because people didn't know whether her womb was now 'unclean', and not suitably pristine for a lawful husband. Many women were ejected from their homes because they had become reproductively useless. Even as late as the 1970's, the idea of womb-purity concerned Turkish migrant workers in Sweden, where they were interviewed by Ullabritt

Engelbrektsson: "Foreign seed ... that is seed from any other than a woman's husband contaminates the field forever making the woman permanently defiled." Perhaps they think another man's seed can lay dormant in the 'field' of her womb, and spring into life many years later, a kind of resurrected ghost-baby. Such reproductive ignorance is a real problem to widows in Nepal and elsewhere today because, even though they're young and healthy, no man will marry them.

A major concern for men has long been the chastity of wives. In the male-seed way of thinking, it was not 50% the woman's child. It was either 100% the husband's, or 100% the child of the man with whom his wife was adulterous. This stark difference led to male paranoia and female punishment on a huge scale. In ancient Egypt, adulterous wives were burnt to death; while in ancient Rome they were stoned to death. The Cheyenne had another fate for their adulterous wives – rape by thirty or forty men. In India today, they continue with the ancient practice of cutting off the nose of a woman suspected of adultery. And in the Near East, Middle East, and Far East, 'honour killings' are still taking place on a daily basis. The idea that a father, husband, or brother can, indeed should, control a woman's sexuality is very deeply entrenched in many cultures. The whole society expects men to beat women, even to death, if there's doubt about her virginity or faithfulness to her husband. This is an inevitable outcome of thinking the woman has no reproductive rights; that her sexuality is not in fact hers; that she is a baby-making machine for a man approved of, or chosen by, her father.

In cultures that are still steeped in male-seed traditions, women are controlled to an upsetting degree. It seems very unjust to us in the developed world where women today are legally free of male constraints. But we forget that we too had to battle against many unequal laws to achieve justice. For example, a British man has always been able to divorce his wife for adultery, but a woman couldn't even apply for a divorce on the grounds of her husband's adultery until 1923.

SELECTED REFERENCES:
Engelbreksson, Ullabritt, *The Force of Tradition: Turkish migrants at home and abroad*, Gothenburg: Acta/University of Gothenburg, 1978, page 137.

8: GENDER POLARITY: CONFIRMED BY SCIENCE

Men of science were unwilling to lift women to equal reproductive status with men, and only succumbed when they had absolutely no choice. They seemed to think their role was to confirm other scientific and philosophical texts that had for thousands of years sent out this message: in the relay-race of life, men pass the baton from father to son, down the generations, forever. In different ways, they all made the same point: reproductively, men and women are profoundly different.

In the male-seed/female-field theory:	
Male seed provides:	**Women provide:**
1) The blueprint or design for the human form. 2) The force, energy or impetus for growth. 3) The spirit. 4) The 'sentient soul' – the thinking, creative ability. 5) The family line or heritage: the link with the past, and with the future.	1) The flesh and blood ('matter').

Over the years there would be discussion about whether the 'matter' women provided to build up the body of the baby came from her menstrual blood, placental blood, sexual secretions or ovarian material. Essentially, though, she provided the *stuff* the body was made with.

The male scientists came up with all kinds of bizarre reasons to explain women's essential reproductive inferiority. They 'proved' it from her anatomy, using any part of her to justify their theory – including her womb, blood, ovaries, ovum, abdominal veins, vagina, the shape of her abdomen, her lack of facial hair, her 'missing five ounces' of brain weight, and even by the fact that she seldom goes bald. There was never a shortage of theories, and they were used not only to explain her second-class 'nature', but her role in life – homebody and male helpmate.

A giant of late 18th century European science was Erasmus Darwin – grandfather of Charles Darwin. He accepted that "The process of generation is still involved in impenetrable obscurity" but nevertheless came to this conclusion: "I contend that the mother does not contribute to the formation of the living ens [the being] in animal generation, but is necessary only for supplying its nutriment and oxygenation." He arrived at this decision after applying a great deal of logic to the question, including this: "the male in many animals is larger, stronger, and digests more food than the female, and therefore should contribute as much or more towards the reproduction of the species." Clearly, a woman carries the baby within her for nine months, gives birth to it, and feeds it from her breasts, so makes a large contribution, but men like Darwin thought there had to be something bigger, and more important, that men did. And there was only one thing left for them to appropriate to themselves – the seed of life itself.

This polarised concept of reproduction suited the men of science. Apparently they enjoyed being viewed as the active, creative, spiritual gender (while women just provided material warmth and sustenance at home) because they fought to maintain this so-called 'natural', biological, division of labour using every trick in the book to confirm it. That is, they hijacked every new scientific discovery they could lay their hands on.

When the First Law of Thermodynamics was formulated by Faraday in 1831, it was used to justify women's role as the nutritive domestic helpmate. The argument was that as "thought and physical energy are mutually-convertible" and as women's childbearing role was so energy depleting, women should not expend energy on mental pursuits because there wouldn't be enough energy left for making and nurturing babies. Education for women would weaken the race.

The road to reproductive truth began in 1827, with the discovery of the mammalian ovum – in a dog. But nothing changed overnight. In fact, the great men of science, using their brilliant logical minds, concluded that if the ovary contained food for the growing baby, then an ovum, inside the ovary, was like an item of shopping in the shopping basket. It would take many decades for the truth to emerge and, meanwhile, men continued to find reasons for women's inferiority.

By the 1880's it was becoming clear that science was going to have to accept the fact that women, being female mammals, have ova which contribute directly to reproduction. This didn't stop the scientific sexism. What they now aimed to do was find ways to use reproductive biology to explain why men will always be more intelligent than, and superior to, women.

For W.K. Brooks, author of *The Law of Heredity* in 1883, the keyword was "variability." He said there were more male idiots, and the geniuses were all men - consequently, men were more "variable," while women were mediocre. He also said, "One of the most remarkable and suggestive of the laws of variation" was that the exclusively male parts were "very much more variable" than the female parts. He didn't say whether he meant that penises differ from one another in size and shape, or whether they are variable because each individual penis can change its size and shape – when erect or not. He also compared the sperm and ovum, and wrote "the male element is the originating and the female the perpetuating factor; the ovum is the conservative, the male cell progressive." Did this affect the brain? You bet:

"... if the female organism is the conservative organism, to which is intrusted the keeping of all that has been gained during the past history of the race, it must follow that the female mind is a storehouse filled with the instincts, habits, intuitions, and laws of conduct which have been gained by past experience. The male organism, on the contrary, being the variable organism, the originating element in the process of evolution, the male mind must have the power of extending experience over new fields and, by comparison and generalization, of discovering new laws of nature ..."

In other words, nature designed men to be scientific geniuses. In 1889 Sir Patrick Geddes and J. Arthur Thomson, writing in *The Evolution of Sex*, came to the same conclusion, this time using the keywords "katabolic" and "anabolic":

"It is generally true that the males are more active, energetic, eager, passionate, and variable; the females more passive, conservative, sluggish, and stable. The males ... the more katabolic organisms ... are more frequently the leaders in evolutionary progress, while the more anabolic females tend rather to preserve the constancy and integrity of the species ... The more active males, with a consequently wider range of experience, may have bigger brains and more intelligence."

All this so-called 'science' served to reassure other men that there was, after all, some basis for their long-held notion they were superior to women. No doubt it was talked about in the exclusively male scientific clubs. We know now that it was all ignorant nonsense, but for women of the time it created a huge barrier to their intellectual and social development.

SELECTED REFERENCES:

Darwin, Erasmus, *Zoonomia or the Laws of Organic Life, Vol. 1*, Dublin: P. Byrne and W. Jones, 1794, quotes from pages, in order, 548, 552 and 549.

Brooks, William Keith, *The Law of Heredity*, Baltimore: John Murphy, 2nd Ed. 1883, pages 160 and 257.

Geddes, Sir Patrick, Thomson, J. Arthur, *The Evolution of Sex*, London: Walter Scott, 1889, pages 270-271.

9: RELIGION

The language of religious texts reflects the ancient male-seed concept of life. In the Hindu text 'The Atharva Veda' it says: "In the male indeed grows the seed. That is poured along into the women." In 'The Book of Manu', which is an important Hindu book of laws pertaining to religious practice, the following verses are found:

"By the sacred tradition the woman is declared to be the soil, the man is declared to be the seed; the production of all corporeal beings (takes place) through the union of the soil with the seed." (9:33)

The text makes it clear that the form of the child, the offspring, is determined not by the womb, yet alone any ovum that may be found there, but by the male seed:

"On comparing the seed and the receptacle (of the seed), the seed is declared to be more important; for the offspring of all created beings is marked by the characteristics of the seed.

Whatever kind on seed is sown in a field, prepared in due season, (a plant) of that same kind, marked with the peculiar qualities of the seed, springs up in it.

This earth, indeed, is called the primeval womb of created beings; but the seed develops not in its development any properties of the womb.

In this world seeds of different kinds, sown at the proper time in the land, even in one field, come forth (each) according to its kind.

The rice (called) vrihi and (that called) sali, mudga-beans, sesamum, masha-beans, barley, leeks, and sugar-cane, (all) spring up according to their seed.

That one (plant) should be sown and another be produced cannot happen; whatever seed is sown, (a plant of) that kind even comes forth." (9:35-40)

In the Qur'an (2:223) men are told "Women are your fields; go, then, into your fields when you please." No doubt this sentence was interpreted differently in the past to how it is today in biologically educated societies, but anthropology shows us that in some places it is still understood to mean that the father provides the seed that is planted in the seedless woman.

There should be a huge difference between accounts of how God made the first humans, and accounts of how humans reproduce, but people have extrapolated from the former to arrive at the latter. In the Qur'an (23:12-14) God made man in the following way:

"We created man of an extraction of clay
then We set him, a drop, in a receptacle secure,
then We created of the drop a clot
then We created of the clot a tissue
then We created of the tissue bones
then We garmented the bones in flesh;
thereafter we produced him as another creature.
So blessed be God, the fairest of creators! …"

This sequence of events is remarkably similar to the "genesis of the embryo" as described by Mehmet Raghib, an 18th century Islamic scholar in *Safinat al-raghib wa dafinat al-matalib* (*The History of Knowledge*). Here, instead of "a drop in a receptacle secure," we have "sperm…placed in the uterus":

"Learned men declare that sperm, when placed in the uterus, is first transformed into a small, round ball, while keeping its original white

colour. And this lasts for six days. At the centre of this ball then appears a spot of blood. This spot will be the confluence of the soul (multaqa al arwah). When the creation is completed this will be the heart ..."

In the Old Testament Book of Job 10:10, God is asked, "Hast thou not poured me out as milk, and curdled me like cheese?" This refers to the 'milk and rennet' theory, which was also given as an analogy for conception by Aristotle in the 4th century BC, and which can still be heard in many parts of the world today. The Jewish Midrash Rabbah (14, 19) explains it thus:

"A mother's womb is full of standing blood, which flows therefrom in menstruation. But, at God's will, a drop of whiteness enters and falls into its midst and behold a child is formed. This is likened unto a bowl of milk; when a drop of rennet falls into it, it congeals and stands; if not it continues as liquid."

Aristotle believed "the active elements" – in this case rennet – were "more divine," and no doubt countless others, before and after him, followed the same reasoning. All the male-seed, male-active theories – whether seed and soil, no ram=no lamb, chicken and egg, or milk and rennet – lead to the same notion: men have the creative spark and women do not. The non-creativity of women, their definition as "matter," stuff for the creative male to work with, distanced women from God in a very profound way. This is how the divine hierarchy looked:

THE CREATIVE GOD

The 'little god' – man

↓

↓

The non-godly – woman

This distance between god and women is reflected in the way religion is dominated by men. Changes have only recently taken place in the Church of England (CofE), which allowed the first ordination of a female vicar in 1994, the first consecration of a female Bishop in January 2015, and the first Senior Bishop in July 2015. However, as the mother church of the Anglican Communion, a fellowship of different Churches in 165 countries, the CofE is facing deep objections to these changes and the possibility that the Communion will break up. Many theologians maintain that women bishops are contrary to the scriptures, but they were written at a time when everyone believed in the idea of a single, male-seed of life and, at the same time, male superiority, and the male-more-divine concept. They understood it to be the 'nature' of men and, because God designed that 'nature', it seemed blasphemous to challenge it. We now know that understanding of 'nature' was a huge mistake.

Jesus himself wasn't against Mary Magdalene joining his inner circle. It was Simon Peter who complained "let Mary leave us, for women are not worthy of life" (Gospel of Thomas 114). This might just seem like a little unfriendliness but Simon Peter thought, like everyone else around at the time, that Mary was, literally, not worthy of life. In other words, God had deemed her, a woman, unworthy of the honour of carrying the seed of life, the creative spark, within her. Jesus retorted "I myself shall lead her, in order to make her male, so she shall become a living spirit, like you males. For every woman who makes herself male will enter the Kingdom of Heaven." However, Jesus went much further in teaching that gender is an illusion and a spiritual irrelevance, judging from his very metaphysical statement in Thomas: 22, "When you make the two into one, and make the inner as the outer, and the outer as the inner, and the above as the below, so the male and female are made into a single One, in order that the male is not made male, nor the female made female: ... then will you enter the Kingdom."

One of the arguments made against women taking high office in the Christian Church is that they are not 'in likeness' to Jesus. What exactly does this expression mean? You can take it in two ways: in terms of masculine physique – the most distinguishing feature of which is the penis; or in terms of creativity – the ability to give life. They are, of course, one and the same thing because the penis is that which delivers male creativity – the life-giving seed. We now know that women too have life-giving seed and are part of the creative dynamic, just like men.

It is striking when reading the Bible that genealogy runs from father to son. There were seventy-four generations from Adam to Jesus, all along the male-seed line. The list is given in *Luke* 3:23-38, working backwards in time and starting with Jesus: "(as was supposed) the son of Joseph." Joseph was the son of Heli, the son of Matthat, and so on through Levi, Melki, Jannai, Joseph, Mattathias, Amos, Nahum, Esli, Naggai, Maath, Mattathias, Semein, Joseph, Joda, Joanan, Rhesa, Zerubbabel, Shealtiel, Neri, Malki, Addi, Cosam, Elmadam, Er, Joshua, Eliezer, Jorim, Matthat, Levi, Simeon, Judah, Joseph, Jonam, Eliakim, Melea, Menna, Mattatha, Nathan, David, Jesse, Obed, Boaz, Salmon, Nahshon, Amminadab, Ram, Hezron, Perez, Judah, Jacob, Isaac, Abraham, Terah, Nahor, Serug, Reu, Peleg, Eber, Shelah, Cainan, Arphaxad, Shem, Noah, Lamech, Methuselah, Enoch, Jared, Mahalaleel, Cainan, Enos and Seth, until we get to Adam, who was created by God.

There are no mothers on this list because they're reproductively irrelevant. They were invisible vessels for the male seed to grow up in. As women didn't contribute any seed material, in a genealogy nobody needed to record who they were.

In the Biblical life-view, men begat and women bore, starting in *Genesis* 5, when Adam begat Seth. The language of the Bible seems to indicate a difference between men, who are "sons of God," and women who are "daughters of men." So, for example, in *Genesis* 6:1, we read "when men began to multiply on the face of the earth, and daughters were born unto them" and in 6:4 "the sons of God came in unto the daughters of men, and they bare children to them."

In the Adam and Eve story, Eve is made out of Adam's rib. This idea, that women proceed from the body of men is echoed in Corinthians 11:7-9, where we learn why a man should not cover his head in church: "he is in the image and glory of God: but the woman is the glory of the man; For the man is not of the woman; but the woman of the man."

To people who thought that men carry the only seed of human life, it was obvious they got it from their fathers, who got it from their fathers, who got it from their fathers. If you carry the logic back to the beginning of time, it becomes inevitable that the original creative force, God, will be perceived as male.

Also, if you think that God gave men the ability to create life, and did not give women that same capacity, you're going to think God has chosen the male gender as more responsible and superior. As only men provide the spark of life, it seems that the essential divinity of creation was theirs alone. This mistake robbed women of their right to spiritual equality, and gave us a spiritual apartheid that continues to this day.

SELECTED REFERENCES:
The Gospel of Thomas is one of fifty-two texts found in a large sealed earthenware jar in Egypt in 1945, known collectively as the Nag Hammadi Library. The Gospel of Thomas is dated between the 1st and 2nd centuries.

10: SO WHY HAS THERE NEVER BEEN A FEMALE BACH OR BEETHOVEN?

The male-seed, female-field, way of thinking placed men and women, as a result of their (incorrect) biology and 'nature', into two completely different categories of human beings:

MEN	WOMEN	The Logical, 'Natural,' Conclusion for Women
Able to create life	Unable to create life	Women are not creative.
Able to create life = god-like = spiritual	Unable to create life = unlike god = non spiritual	Women are not spiritual; Women excluded from spiritual leadership.
Sentient soul – thinking person	Not a sentient soul – incapable of deep intellectual thought	Women excluded from intellectual activity.
Superior	Inferior	Women not respected.
Chastity not important	Chastity vital	Women unable to move freely from place to place.
Reproduces; source of future generations	Does not reproduce = has no reproductive rights; has no right to refuse man his right to reproduce	Women's sexuality controlled by men.
Biological inheritance leads to property inheritance	Biological lack of inheritance leads to lack of property inheritance	Women have few financial resources; women beholden to men to pay for them.
Free to move from place to place	Not free to move from place to place	Women can't get a job away from home.

Reproducer helped by woman	Non-reproducer who helps the man reproduce	Woman is defined as 'the helper' or 'helpmeet'.
Parent – decides child's fate in present	Not a parent	Woman can't decide child's fate in present.
Parent – decides child's fate in future	Not a parent	Woman can't decide child's future fate.
Has a future through his children	Evolutionary dead-end	Future is not woman's; she has no rights or say in it.
Future is his – can get involved in local and national politics	Future is not hers – can't get involved in local and national politics	Women excluded from political activity.

From the list on the right you can see that the male-seed, female-field, way of thinking made it almost inevitable that women would be excluded from spiritual leadership, intellectual activity, and political activity, because of a set of 'facts' of life that were completely wrong. Women didn't generally fight to be included in these male areas of activity because, like men, they too thought they were different to men, and not their equals.

Because of the chastity issue, women simply didn't have the freedom to move about the place. They couldn't sit around with a group of males and discuss the nature of the universe unless they had a chaperone with them. A woman couldn't be alone with one man, yet alone a group of them, and she couldn't attend any meetings in other towns, out of sight of her protective father and brothers. A man, on the other hand, could jump on a horse or a boat and go wherever he liked. He was free; she was not. Any woman alone on the road was suspected of being a whore.

Women were defined as non-creative, non-spiritual, and non-intellectual. A woman who broke this mould would be considered an intellectual transvestite. It wasn't expected, and it wasn't 'natural', as God had apparently designed it. Breaking the mould could be seen as blasphemous. A woman who dared to attempt creativity was going 'above herself' or 'not knowing her place'. A woman might be able to play the harpsichord very well, but she would have to play music written by a man. She was allowed to copy, but not create.

A big problem was the sheer weight of opposition she faced from innumerable influential social commentators. One of these was an American, John Todd, author of the 19th century best sellers *A Student's Manual* and *Women's Rights*. He wrote "...have you never seen the girl thumping and drumming her piano for years, under the best teachers, and yet her brother come along and take it up, and without any teaching, soon go in advance of the sister? I have seen it often." This sexist attitude had been around for centuries and no doubt contributed to any lack of self-confidence and self-esteem that women felt.

There were also practical issues to consider. All the great artists and musicians needed patrons, people who employed them, usually church leaders, kings or princes. The artist or composer would have to live in the court, or nearby, and create works of art or music for their patron. If a woman wanted to go to Florence to paint a portrait, her father would be unlikely to allow it because he didn't want her arrogant, upstart, flightiness to bring shame on the family. Her mother, brothers and sisters would all feel the same. Aside from which, no patron would commission work from her because, as everyone knew, women were not creative.

We have to remember in all this that it wasn't just men who thought they were the only creative, thinking, creatures. Women too thought this, as did young men, young women, boys and girls. The 'natural' polarity was instilled into people from an early age.

Yes, there were a few female painters who created great works of art, but they usually did it in their father's atelier, or workshop. And there was some scope for female intellectual activity in the safety of entirely female company – in nunneries, for example. But all the professional guilds and societies excluded women.

Sexist societies constrain women on every front. It's like the women are in a maze with no exit. They can turn this way and that, but there's no way out. And marriage may not offer a hand of help. This was the social reality for married women in England in 1850:

The legal position of married women in England, 1850

* Not allowed to own property (any property passed to her husband on their marriage)

* Not allowed to complain about rape within marriage (because not recognised in law)

* Not allowed to keep her wages for work (because they belonged to her husband)

* Not allowed to make a Will (because she owns nothing)

* Not allowed to see her children if husband so decides (because they are *his*)

> * Not allowed to have own business (because she can't make contracts or incur debts)
>
> * Not allowed to divorce (between 1700-1850 only *four* women were granted a divorce)

SELECTED REFERENCES:
Todd, Rev. John D.D., *Women's Rights*, Boston: Lee and Shepard, 1867, page 11.

11: NON-PEOPLE

Women in Canada became 'people' on October 18th 1929 in a legal case known as 'The Person's Case,' brought against the attorney-general of Canada by 'the famous five' – Henrietta Muir Edwards, Nellie McClung, Louise McKinney, Emily Murphy, and Irene Parlby. At the time, Canada was a Dominion of the United Kingdom and Canada's law was enshrined in the British North America Act of 1867, which referred to "men" being allowed to do this and that, using the male noun and pronoun throughout. This linguistic detail was being used by men to prevent women becoming members of the Senate of Canada. Having tried to get a change of wording through the Canadian court without success, the women took their case to London, England, and appealed to the higher court of the Judicial Committee of the Privy Council, who judged that "the word 'persons' in section 24 includes members both of the male and female sex." In law, this was a huge turning point not only for women in Canada, but in the United Kingdom too. The Lord Chancellor, Viscount Sankey, made a statement that is still pertinent today:

"Customs are apt to develop into traditions which are stronger than law and remain unchallenged long after the reason for them has disappeared."

The very fact that 'the famous five' had to fight this case at all shows us there was male resistance to female equality at the time. Men had got used to their superiority over women, and they liked it. Under English common law women had been non-persons. As the 18th century lawyer, Sir William Blackstone, put it: "In law husband and wife are one person, and the husband is that person." In many respects this thinking carried on long after the 1929 ruling. For example, a woman in England couldn't get her own mortgage until the 1960's.

In the world today there are billions of women who are still non-people, to some legal degree or other. A Chinese government web site tells us that the wife "is deemed as no longer part of her own family, but the 'property' of the husband's family." Meanwhile in Islamic areas of the world, Shari'a law considers men legally independent at puberty, but not women. They're under the legal control of their fathers until marriage, when legal control transfers to the husband. In some parts of the world a woman can't get on a train or a plane without the permission of a man – her husband, or father, or brother, or even her son.

To what do we attribute this ridiculous level of male control over women that spread over so much over the world, for so long? Personally I do not subscribe to the theory that men are natural control freaks and thugs, and instead think there must have been a logical reason for it.

Let's now try to put ourselves into the minds of men living with the male-seed way of thinking. You look at a woman - what do you see? You see a creature that God put on earth to receive your seed, hold it in her womb for nine months, feed it from her breast and nurture it. That will be your child. God (nature) designed woman's body to help you reproduce yourself. Her biology defines her as your helper; she is an appendage to you. You feel sorry for her. She has no children of her own, no stake in the future. She stops here. Only you will be recognised as the originating source of the children, their parent or forefather. You feel a sense of expansion; you have a future in your children. And the boys will carry your seed into the future. You look at the woman again. She's an evolutionary dead-end. She's not important. Not like you. God chose to give you the seed. You feel privileged. Superior. Important. It feels nice.

You think about her again. She scares you. What if she has sex with another man? She'll carry his child, not yours. How dare she! She has no reproductive rights because she doesn't reproduce. You are the reproducer; you have the seed. Can you trust her? Can you trust other men? You feel helpless, dependent, and afraid. Now you get angry. You think: I need to control her, keep her away from other men. She's mine, my baby-making machine. She's going inside the house and staying there. Keep her under control, that's the answer. Allow her nothing, let her know her place. She's mine, and I will rule over her.

SELECTED REFERENCES:
The Economic and Commercial Counsellor's Office of the Embassy of the People's Republic of China in the United States of America, http://us2.mofcom.gov.cn/article/aboutchina/custom/200411/20041100004548.shtml. Accessed April 2017.

12: CONJUGAL RIGHTS, RAPE, CHILD ABUSE

If you think of a woman as your baby-making machine, you get the mind-set that once lawfully married, she should make herself available to you. Her womb is your womb. The way to her womb, her vagina, is your vagina, and she can't refuse you access. In other words, if she refuses, you have the right to rape her. In many societies, possibly most societies today, rape within marriage is legal. In Britain, it only became illegal in 1991. As the 16th century Christian leader, Martin Luther, said: "Let them bear children till they die of it ... that is what they are for."

Women who were raped have been stoned to death, divorced, made to marry the rapist, thrown out of the home for bringing 'shame' on the family, or made unmarriageable because they were thought permanently 'defiled'. No doubt many women kept the rape a secret so their family didn't know it had happened.

Rape is about control: men thinking they have the right to control women. We've all seen the statistics; and we all know women who have been raped. Statistically, one in six women reading this have been raped, probably by a man they knew and trusted. Given that historically, for century after century, men have been excused for rape, it's not so surprising that this legacy has seeped into our own time. Men still think they have the right to control women – the statistics prove that. And because in the UK only 6% of reported rapes actually end in a conviction, it appears that society still doesn't punish enough rapists. Women still have to fear men because it is men who are out of control. If men today knew very clearly that they wouldn't get away with it, they wouldn't do it. Instead, they do get away with it, often because the woman doesn't want to go through the legal process and be made to feel the guilty party. So what exactly has changed?

The male-seed theory of reproduction leads directly to the notion that the child is 100% the grown seed of the man. Just as a farmer looks at the crops in his fields and knows he can do whatever he wants with them, a male-seed father looks at the child and says "that's mine." That child came from inside him, his semen, and is now, after a growing period inside a woman, still as much a part of him as, say, his fingers or toes. When a child grows up in a male-seed culture, he or she sees in the father their source, the person to whom they owe their life – the only person they have to obey totally.

Men have abused this control to a phenomenal degree. Taking the world as a whole, research estimates that, each day, as many as 100 million young girls are being sexually abused or raped by their fathers. Day after day. Who knows how many mothers are aware of this, but no doubt many are, and feel they have no say in the matter because the children are the grown seed of the father, and theirs to do with as they wish. In Britain, child abuse is clearly now against the law, but men still do it in secret. This may be the most gruesome manifestation of a tradition that gave men total rights over children.

13: A RESEMBLANCE TO MOTHER

Before people knew about the female seed, the ovum, how was a resemblance between mother and child explained? The simplest and most usual answer was that seeds develop differently depending on the soil in which they're grown. A child may look like its mother simply because it grew inside her and was nourished by her. This was essentially the answer given to the question by 18th century Dutch professor of medicine, Hermann Boerhaave. He was so famous that the postman was able to deliver a letter sent to him by a Chinese mandarin, addressed simply "To the illustrious Boerhaave, physician in Europe." This was Boerhaave's explanation:

"The father communicates the embryo and first rudiments of life, the structure of the body being already determined and assigned in the animalcules of the male semen in all creatures, which yet receives some alteration according to the different species of animal or female from whence it is nourished."

How this "alteration" came about was a matter of debate. In 1714, French physician Nicolas Andry suggested that "uterine juices," possibly meaning amniotic fluid, influenced the look of the child. In 1740 French professor of medicine Jean Astruc was teaching that a sperm pushes into a pore or passage in the ovum and as it did so was "shaped, and, as it were, moulded; whence it is more or less stamped to the likeness of its mother ..." Astruc sounds radical in hypothesising an ovum (which wasn't discovered in mammals until 1827), but he thought of it simply as a safe resting place for the sperm, complete with a door (or passage) that closed, once the lucky sperm was inside. Charles Darwin believed in "pangenesis," which imagined there were "gemmules" floating in the bloodstream of both parents, which picked up characteristics and transmitted them to the child.

Given that the foetus spends nine months inside the woman's body, there was plenty of scope to hypothesise why a child looked like it's mother, from the general – like 'movements of diverse humors', to the particular – her womb, her amniotic fluid, her venal blood, her menstrual blood, her non-generative 'seed', her 'sexual secretions', her placenta, and so on. And if you weren't convinced by any of these, there was always her mind.

Around 440 BC, the Greek philosopher Empedocles thought the mother's imagination was so powerful it could guide the formation of the embryo and interfere with it. Over the centuries the rather vague term 'the force of the mother's imagination' was used repeatedly, although people meant a variety of things by it. Some said the child looked like the mother if she particularly wanted a child at the time of intercourse; others said the child looked like her if she was particularly desirous of the father when the child was conceived; while others said the child looked like its mother if she had been suddenly frightened during early pregnancy. When anthropologist Carol Delaney interviewed a man in Eastern Turkey in the 1980's, she was told the child resembles the mother if she has an orgasm before the man and produces a lot of sexual fluid, while the child resembles the father if he comes first.

There have been many theories as to why children can resemble their mother and, as well as providing support for the basic 'fact' that men provide the seed, they give an opportunity to blame women for anything that goes wrong.

Before the days of sperm counts, semen was analogous with 'seed' and because men produce semen – ejaculate – whether they are barren of sperm or not, women always got the blame for any lack of children. If women produced only daughters, it could be blamed on her imagination, or on her faulty 'nourishment' – as if her 'soil' was imperfect. In 1685 Swiss anatomist Johann Conrad Peyer blamed the occurrence of monster-children on the force of the mother's imagination or the machinations of 'the Devil', saying the baby was deformed as a punishment for sin. And you can guess who got the blame for sinning.

SELECTED REFERENCES:
Boerhaave, Hermann, quoted in Cole, F. J., *Early Theories of Sexual Generation*, Oxford: Clarendon Press, 1930, pages 84-85.
Jean Astruc, *A Treatise on all the Diseases Incident to Women*, London, 1743.
Cole, Francis Joseph, *Early Theories of Sexual Generation*, Oxford: Clarendon Press, 1930, p84.
Needham, Joseph, *A History of Embryology*, Cambridge: Cambridge University Press, 1959, p29.
Delaney, Carol, *The Seed and the Soil: Gender and Cosmology in Turkish Village Society*, page 46, © 1994 by the Regents of the University of California. Published by the University of California Press.

14: WOMEN LIBERATED FROM INCUBATOR STATUS

I'm looking at a huge 21st century reference book, with 630 large-format pages packed full of interesting information to do with history and science. It tells me the can opener was invented in 1934 – fascinating. But it tells me absolutely nothing about the discovery of the basic facts of human reproduction – there is ovum and sperm and fusion. It jumps straight to genetics and DNA. Hallo? What happened to the bit where men thought they were the only parents? Or was it just a minor incidental of history that women were considered incubators for male seed for thousands of years? No wonder everyone I meet thinks "people have always known the facts of life." Nobody told them any different.

Instead, we are led to believe there was some logical reason for men's obvious domination of the world for the last few thousand years. We call it "tradition," without any idea that its foundations were laid upon a huge and profound error of information that affected men and women deeply. The male-seed theory of reproduction was the mortar that kept the towers of patriarchy together, and because we can't see that the mortar has, in fact, crumbled, the towers remain intact – toppling, but still in place.

Every single child ever born asks "where do I come from?" And it's amazing that all children throughout historic time, and millions of children around the world today, are still given the wrong answer. You'd think that, as this question is so universal, someone might have taken an interest in noting the point at which the true facts of life became known. But you need to be an expert in the history of embryology to know we had the 'facts' of life utterly wrong for so long.

This may be the biggest cover-up of all time. Was it a conscious conspiracy, with men of science whispering around corners in their exclusive male clubs saying 'Look, let's just pretend we always knew', or was it a subconscious thing? In either case, you can see why the cover-up happened – men didn't want to admit their ever-so-comfortable superiority was based on a big mistake.

So let's just run through some of the long list of important discoveries that led to the discovery of the facts of life. I've noted the animals the work was carried out on because during these years there were still people who wanted to believe that human beings (especially male human beings) bore no relation whatsoever to the lowly little creatures the experiments were carried out on. Consequently, they denied that the experiments had anything to do with *them*.

DATE	ANIMAL	SCIENTIST/S	DISCOVERY
1824	Frogs	Jean-Louis Prevost & Jean-Baptiste Dumas	Egg fertilised by sperm.
1827	Dog	Karl Ernst von Baer	Mammalian ovum observed.
By 1847	Frogs, newts, fish, starfish, hydrozoa, birds, rabbits	Various	Division observed in fertilised eggs.
1853	Frogs	George Newport	Sperm seen to penetrate egg.
1861	Vertebrate/s	Carl Gegenbaur	Ovum is unicellular.
1873	Iso-turbellarian worms	Friedrich Anton Schneider	Observes the nucleus in division (mitosis) in cells of cleaving eggs.
[1875] [1880] (1884)	[Rabbits] and (bats)	Edouard van Beneden	Detailed description of blastocyst.

Year	Organism	Researcher	Finding
1876	Sea urchins	Oskar Hertwig	Recognised that the essential factor in fertilisation is the fusion of sperm and ovum nuclei.
1877	Starfish	Hermann Fol	Observed that a single sperm causes fertilisation.
1885		Rudolf Albert von Kolliker	Described sperm as cellular in origin and nature and postulated that hereditary characteristics are transmitted by the cell nucleus.
1885-1892		August Weismann	"germ plasm" theory – anticipated chromosomal basis of inheritance.
1888	Parasitic worms *Ascaris megalo-cephala*	Theodor Boveri	Shows that shape and arrangement of chromosomes is the same in cells before and after cell division.
1890	Sea urchins		Discovers sperm and egg contributes equal number of sets of chromosomes.
1891	Insects (*Pyrrhocoris Apterus*)	Hermann Henking	Described accessory chromosomes.

1900: re-discovered 35 years after writing	Garden peas	Gregor Mendel	Hereditary traits such as size and colour shown to pass down generations.
1902	Insects (*Acridian genus Hippiscus*)	C.E. McClung	Chromosomes determinants of gender.
1909		Wilhelm Johannsen	Coined the terms 'gene', 'genotype', and 'phenotype'
1915	Fruit fly Drosophila	Thomas Hunt Morgan	Shows identifiable, hereditary information is located in chromosomes.
1953		James Watson and Francis Crick	Discovered double-helix structure of DNA in chromosomes. Showed how DNA can copy itself, passing on genetic information.
1956	Humans	Joe Hin Tjio and Albert Levan	Showed that normal number of chromosomes in humans is 46.
1960	Humans	Landrum Shettles	Photo-micrographic proof of sperm entering ovum in humans.

15: MY HERO

My hero is Estonian scientist Karl Ernst von Baer who, one fine spring day in 1827, discovered the mammalian ovum, in a dog. This discovery made it possible to come up with an accurate explanation of human reproduction but it would take another one hundred and thirty three years to reach experimental proof, in 1960. It was a long journey involving dozens of scientists in many different kinds of experimentation. Although these others carried out important work in finding out how sea urchins and other small slimy animals reproduced, what everyone was interested in is how *human* reproduction worked.

Scientists had been looking for the mammalian ovum for centuries, but had not been able to find it. Von Baer found it, and made it possible to speculate that human females have a seed. This was revolutionary – and not what men wanted to hear. Von Baer knew this. And he was himself shocked. He wrote in his autobiography of the moment he looked down his microscope in Königsberg, and saw the ovum:

"Taking a single look through the instrument, I recoiled as if struck by lightning, because I saw a small, well-defined yellow yolk mass. I had to try to relax a while before I could work up enough courage to look again, as I was afraid that I had been deluded by a phantom. Is it not strange that a sight which is expected, and indeed hoped for, should be frightening when it eventually materializes?"

Strange indeed. This was the 'Eureka!' moment in reproduction history. You'd think everyone would have gathered around von Baer and patted him on the back. That would have happened if women were working in science at the time, but in 1827 all the scientists were men. Women weren't allowed into the lab or into the scientific establishments. Their role had already been defined as the nurturing homemaker. So how did the men of science react? They turned their backs on von Baer and pretended it hadn't happened.

Von Baer wrote up his discovery in a scientific paper called *De Ovi Mammalium et Hominis Genesi Epistola* and sent it to many of the key players in the field. But they ignored it, as did everyone else, and the paper didn't sell. In fact, it sold so badly his publisher declined to publish his next work. As von Baer recalls in his autobiography, his discovery was met by *"altum silentum"* – silence. "That the older men would not read my paper or, at least, would not let it shake their convictions, I could well imagine. But that the younger participants, also remained silent – that I found disturbing."

Eighteen months after the discovery, in September 1828, von Baer attended a scientific conference in Berlin. He wrote:

"... not a single one of the anatomists with whom I became acquainted even so much as mentioned my paper. The paper had been made available to the public as early as the middle of January, and it was highly unlikely that no one had heard of it, especially as I had taken care to have it sent to some of them ... I was too proud or too vain to bring up the subject myself in Berlin. Was my work regarded as a joke or a gross mistake? Or was the subject matter itself of too minor an importance to bother about? I really and truly did not know."

The participants at the conference knew perfectly well the significance of von Baer's discovery and, indeed, that their own dearly-held theories would have to change. Then, on the last day, one bold delegate came forward and asked the question he and everyone else had on their minds: "Could you not show us the mammalian ovum in the ovary." Von Baer willingly agreed and the janitor of the anatomical institute hurried off to prepare his female dog for the "sacrifice." "A rather large number of anatomists" excitedly decamped to the dissection room, where von Baer duly provided the evidence. By the end of the afternoon, wrote von Baer, "as far as I could make out, everybody seemed convinced, although I am certain that they had been rather doubtful earlier."

Even this public confirmation of von Baer's discovery was not enough, however, to sway the scientific community at large, and for years much-respected scientists chose to ignore it. Von Baer began to get depressed. More than that, according to Arthur William Meyer, von Baer became "distressed, distraught, spiritless and emaciated, and suffered constantly from nostalgia." He was remembering the good times – before he made his discovery and became the pariah of the male-dominated scientific world. Von Baer wrote that he had become a hermit crab who never left his home. He was gripped with "a despondency" that was in part attributable to "moral grounds" and felt a "mood of dejection" partly caused by "spiritual factors." His work had certainly opened up moral and spiritual dilemmas, and von Baer also realised that the discovery of the mammalian ovum challenged everything previously written about the superiority of men in terms of reproduction. For years men of science cold-shouldered von Baer, even though he wasn't actually daring enough to propose ovum and sperm fusion:

"Perhaps later we shall yet succeed in proving that the formative relations of the germinal vesicula and the spermatic animalcules (ovum and sperm) correspond. We believe to have found a faint trace of the path to this secret. At present, however, it is still so dark and so little persued that we do not dare risk proposing it."

There wasn't going to be a revolution overnight!

SELECTED REFERENCES:
Baer, Karl Ernst von, *Autobiography of Dr. Karl Ernst von Baer*, (ed. Jane M. Oppenheimer), Canton, MA: Watson Publishing International, 1986, quotes from pages, in order, 218, 225, 226, and 269.
Meyer, Arthur William, *Human Generation, Conclusions of Burdach, Dollinger and von Baer*, Palo Alto: Stanford University Press, 1956, page 73, and quoting von Baer on page 117.

16: THE FAILED OVUM-SEEKERS

Karl Ernst von Baer found the mammalian ovum and guaranteed his place in scientific history. Many others had spent years trying, unsuccessfully, to find the same thing. Von Baer attributed his luck to two things – his poor eyesight, and the decision to look for the ovum in a dog. He wore thick glasses and fell about the place but, as he wrote, "My eyes, which because of their near-sightedness have caused me many an awkward moment in every-day situations, have given me excellent service during anatomical research in that they made small pictures quite clear."

William Harvey, the man who discovered blood circulation, stated his theory in 1651, that *omne vivum ex ovo* – all animals are produced from eggs. The problem was he couldn't prove it, despite having access to all the deer in the hunting parks of King Charles 1. And even if he had found the ovum, he had already made up his mind that it was the male who contributed an invisible ("incorporeal") "fructifying power."

Through the ages 'the ovum' was a term applied to various parts of the female anatomy incorrectly, and was anyway thought to be non-generative, or generative only of less important parts. In 1740 French professor of medicine Jean Astruc was talking about a female 'egg' being responsible for the formation of the placenta and membranes – which was a popular theory at the time.

The ovaries had been known about since the ancient Egyptians, but the question always was 'what are they for?' Galen, the ancient Greek anatomist, thought they were the source of secretions produced during sexual excitement:

"... this liquid not only stimulates to the sexual act but also gives pleasure and moistens the passageway as it escapes. It manifestly flows from women as they experience the greatest pleasure in coitus, when it is perceptibly shed upon the pudendum; indeed, such an outflow seems to give a certain pleasure even to eunuchs."

Galen thought that this liquid, which he called "seed," was expelled from the ovaries during sexual excitement, rather as sperm is ejaculated. However, that's where the similarity ends because, according to Galen, the female seed "contributes nothing to the generation of offspring."

In 1672, in the pretty canal town of Delft in Holland, a young surgeon called Regnier de Graaf discovered, in a rabbit, what he thought was the ovum. It was in fact the sac that contains the ovum, within the ovary, now known as the Graafian follicle. It was not this anatomical inaccuracy, however, that prevented the newly discovered 'egg' from being seen as the generative female seed. For centuries, many scientists thought the ovaries contained food for the baby growing in the uterus. When de Graaf found an 'egg', it was seen as a detail of this basic scenario: the ovary is a shopping bag full of supplies for the foetus, and the 'egg' is a sub-unit – an item of shopping.

One man, 125 years later, who thought de Graaf had been onto something more substantial was William Cruikshank, an anatomy teacher in Edinburgh. He wrote of de Graaf that he "had the fate of Cassandra, to be disbelieved even when he spoke the truth." Cruikshank got himself some rabbits, and in 1797 discovered 29 rabbit ova. Unfortunately for him and for science, he was an alcoholic, and nobody believed a word he said.

The most important anatomist and physiologist of the 18th century was Albrecht von Haller who, in the 1750's, cut up 40 sheep in vain, looking for an ovum. He was working with the theory that intercourse caused a fluid to be released from inside the woman, into her womb, where it coagulated into an ovum. This same theory was outlined in the classic textbook of 1826, *Physiology* by Burdach.

The centuries rolled by, and eminent men of science came and went, but the same old question remained – 'how is reproduction achieved?' But were they ready for the answer? As poor von Baer discovered to his mental and emotional cost, even when he proved the existence of the mammalian ovum to his professional peers, it would take them decades to get over the shock.

SELECTED REFERENCES:
Baer, Karl Ernst von, *Autobiography of Dr. Karl Ernst von Baer,* (ed. Jane M. Oppenheimer), Canton, MA: Watson Publishing International, 1986, page 222.

17: THE MAN WITH THE PEAS

It would be nice to have an exact date to say 'this is when we discovered the facts of human reproduction,' but as it took one hundred and thirty three years from start to finish, it's not that easy. The start was 1827 when the mammalian ovum was discovered and a correct hypothesis could be formulated, and the finish was 1960 when photos proved that human reproduction was essentially the same as that of sea urchins. In the 1800's people were generally reluctant to say anything that conflicted with what was outlined in the Bible. For Charles Darwin to say we were descended from apes took a lot of courage because in Genesis 1:26 "God said, Let us make man in our image, after our likeness: and let them have dominion over the fish … the fowl … and the cattle …." In this reality, human beings are very distinct from, and superior to, animals – not evolved from them.

Embryological research was very disturbing because it showed (erroneous) 'proof' that at the foetal stage of life human beings were pretty much indistinguishable from frogs, pigs and many other animals. We seemed to share a family resemblance and people didn't like it. The experiments that slowly made the facts of life known were being carried out on rabbits, starfish, sea urchins, frogs, newts, bats, parasitic worms and fruit flies, so people were very reluctant to accept these discoveries had anything to do with *them* - the vastly superior human being.

Where, along the 133-year line of discovery, a person decided to accept the emerging truth rather depended on their philosophical opposition to it. You could take your choice. You could dig your heels in and say "I'm nothing like a sea urchin" and refuse to be put in the same category – and people did. For them, it would take visual proof that human reproduction was the same as for these small creatures. Only then would they allow the reality of the situation to sink in. And that came when IVF started, and Dr Landrum Shettles showed, in a petri dish, human sperm entering human ovum and, in 1960, he took a picture of it.

But in the scientific world, they didn't need to wait for Landrum Shettles. They had so much evidence building up, the theory was rock solid long before 1960. If I had to give a date, I'd say 1900. It's a nice round figure, and it's also when the work of Gregor Mendel was rediscovered by three separate people.

Mendel was schoolteacher-monk who grew peas in the sunny walled garden of the St. Thomas monastery in Brunn. In fact, he spent seven years growing generation after generation of them. When he was a student at the Vienna Botanical Gardens, Mendel had a run-in with one of the professors, Eduard Fenzl, who was what is known as a 'spermist'. Fenzl thought the plant embryo was pre-formed, perfect in every detail except miniature, needing only the nurturing aspect of a plant ovary to grow. Mendel, on the other hand, believed that each plant was a new creation from both the male, and female, parts.

The story goes that Mendel decided to prove his teacher wrong. He wanted to show that the female contributes as much as the male to inheritance. He spent seven years doing just that, and wrote about it in 1865. Mendel's Laws, as they became known, are often said to have been left unnoticed for 35 years, until rediscovered in 1900. In fact they were cited in twenty-two scientific works over that time. Mendel carried out an important and revealing piece of meticulous research, but his story shows us, again, that it's one thing to make a discovery, and quite another to have one's contemporaries accept it. In Mendel's case, it would take 35 years before the world would take on board what he was actually saying: the female plant contributes as much, in terms of hereditary traits, as males. Only by 1900 was the world ready to hear it.

That's why I choose 1900 as the date to say 'that's when we knew the facts of life', because the world was then prepared to accept the new reality. At least, most of the world. As far as human reproduction went, there were still some people refusing to believe what science showed them, and they did have a point … we were still only talking about peas.

SELECTED REFERENCES:
Henig, Robin Marantz, *A Monk and Two Peas*, London: Weidenfeld and Nicolson, 2000.

18: SPERM – THE LITTLE ANIMALCULES

Men were convinced the seminal fluid that came out of their penises was the stuff of life, so they were very excited when someone discovered that inside this liquid were little wiggly creatures, sperm. Some 178 years after the discovery, the German zoologist, Rudolf Leuckart, wrote "there is scarcely any discovery in the realm of animal biology which has aroused so general an interest as the discovery of these motile seminal corpuscles." All this, of course, was in stark contrast to the discovery of the mammalian ovum by poor old Karl Ernst von Baer, who was met by *altum silentum* – silence.

Sperm were discovered in 1675 by an uneducated haberdasher in Delft, Holland, called Antoni van Leeuwenhoek. He wanted a microscope so he could more closely examine the weave of the cloth he bought and sold. Microscopes became his hobby, and he was exceptionally good at it, achieving magnification of x300 using a single lens. In the history of magnification he stands alone, as nobody could replicate the magnifying power he achieved until 150 years after his death.

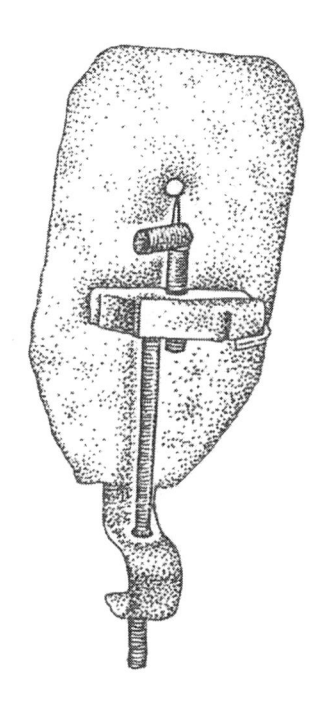

Fig. 1. Microscope made by Antoni van Leeuwenhoek 1675.
Brass, total height 7cm, lens 3mm

Leeuwenhoek's microscopes were tiny, a mere speck of glass embedded in about 3 inches (8cm) of flat, beaten metal, usually brass. A pin at the back held dry specimens in place, while fluids were examined in small glass tubes. Leeuwenhoek first examined bee mouthparts and stings, then progressed to pepper, plaque from teeth, fleas, fungi, water from stagnant pools, blood, and semen. Leeuwenhoek looked at anything and everything. His family and neighbours ridiculed him, and the business suffered, but Leeuwenhoek was a man obsessed.

Although he had no scientific training, Leeuwenhoek had the good sense to make notes of everything he found. He correctly recorded the size of red blood cells relative to bacteria and made important contributions to our understanding of eyes, muscle structure, teeth, and so on. It was all this, as well as the fact that he discovered sperm, that ensured Leeuwenhoek would become known as 'the father of microbiology and protozoology'.

Leeuwenhoek came to the attention of his young neighbour and local surgeon, Regnier de Graaf, who introduced him to the preeminent scientific club, the Royal Society in London. De Graaf had, coincidentally, three years earlier, discovered Graafian follicles (which bear his name), and in which are the ova. His peer group thought they were just items of shopping in the nutritive ovary, food for the growing baby within, so it's an irony that, while de Graaf's work was basically ignored, when he introduced Leeuwenhoek to the scientific community, a furore broke out. Leeuwenhoek immediately became a celebrity, and eminent gentlemen rushed from all over Europe to see for themselves these little discoveries – especially sperm or, 'animalcules', as he called them.

Leeuwenhoek thought that sperm contained the seed of human life, in much the same way that one seed in an apple has the potential to be a whole apple tree, writing that it is "no less improper to say, that the worms in mens' seed are children, tho' children come from them."

Science historian F.J. Cole says that sperm were talked about everywhere and caused a great stir. He wrote:

"The widespread support which animalculism received may be partly explained as the result of subconscious bias. Such a view endorsed the superior status of the male sex, through which alone the distinctive characters of a species were preserved and inherited."

Scientists were desperate to see Leeuwenhoek's exciting tiny world, and wanted him to give them or make them or lend them one of his microscopes. But Leeuwenhoek would not oblige and, instead, he looked down a microscope and declared that he had seen an ovum, and it was definitely non-generative. This lie might have been found out much earlier had it not been for the fact that, on his death, Leeuwenhoek's microscopes got lost or stolen, and because their magnifying power couldn't be replicated for another 150 years, nobody could prove him wrong.

SELECTED REFERENCES:
Leuckart quoted in Cole, F. J., *Early Theories of Sexual Generation*, Oxford: Clarendon Press, 1930, page 1.
Cole, Francis Joseph, *Early Theories of Sexual Generation*, Oxford: Clarendon Press, 1930, pages 207-208. By permission of Oxford University Press, www.oup.com.
Dobell, Clifford, *Anthony von Leeuwenhoek and his Little Animals*, New York: Dover, 1960.

19: LET'S DO WHAT THEY DID

Over the centuries men have had lots of fun 'proving' their superiority by extrapolating from the facts of life as they knew them, or imagined them, or made them up. So let's do the same – but we'll use the actual facts:

MALE Contribution	FEMALE Contribution	CONCLUSION
The sperm is 2.5 um across. By volume, the smallest cell in the body.	The ovum is 100 um across – the largest cell in the body.	***Women contribute more – much more.***
The sperm head (acrosome)	Ovum contains a nucleus with its	Each nucleus contributes 23 chromosomes =

contains a nucleus, with its package of nucleic DNA.	package of nucleic DNA.	the 46 each new life starts with. *Genetic inheritance is equal.*
The sperm nucleus contains RNA (ribonucleic acid)	Ovum nucleus contains RNA.	RNA facilitates cells' copying of DNA. **Both involved in cell replication.**
No cytoplasm.	Ovum contains cytoplasm.	All cytoplasm in zygote, then embryo, comes from mother. *Material of cells comes from mother.*
No mitochondria. The sperm tail has two parts: the middle contains packages of mitochondria; the end part is the flagellum; both fall off before the head enters the ovum. (The mitochondria fuel the flagellum - which provides movement to get to the ovum and, like the middle	Mitochondria in cytoplasm of ovum.	The only mitochondria a person has comes from the woman. Mitochondria are the powerhouses of all cells. They convert glucose into ATP, the fuel for every cell. *Women provide the only source of cell energy, therefore human energy.*

part, plays no active role in reproduction).		
No ribosomes.	Cytoplasm of ovum contains ribosomes.	Ribosomes transform amino acids into proteins. *Female provides essential building blocks of cells.*
No endoplasmic reticulum.	Endoplasmic reticulum in cytoplasm of ovum.	The endoplasmic reticulum provide the transport system inside the cell, moving proteins and other material to their correct places. *Female provides cell's ability to organise itself.*
No Gogli elements	Gogli elements in cytoplasm of ovum.	The Gogli transform proteins into vacuoles, which are membrane-bound bubbles that contain either nutrients, for the cell to use, or waste, for it to expel. *The female contributes the*

> *apparatus for cell nutriment, and also for cell waste. Without it, the cell would not be able to grow, and would poison itself.*

The body of the zygote, which becomes the embryo, comes from the cytoplasm of the ovum. This contains the organs of the cell – the organelles – in the same way that a body contains various organs. Mitochondria are an organelle, and they provide the energy for the cells, while other organelles carry out the work required to keep the cells alive. There are other elements in the ovum, including annulate lamellae, which are thought to be important in terms of the regulation of gene expression, and microvilli, that help absorb nutrients from outside the cell. But I think we have enough to be going on with. Basically, this is the story: the human body has about 37.2 trillion cells and every single one of them grows from material provided by the female contribution, the ovum.

The male provides 'genomic imprinting' (DNA), but so does the female. And the male provides RNA for the cell to replicate, but so does the female. So, all in all, who makes the greater contribution? There's no question about it: the woman contributes more than the man, much more.

20: OTHER THEORIES OF REPRODUCTION

In the Pacific Ocean there are a group of islands where people don't think men have *anything* to do with procreation. Babies are spirits that float on leaves from a particular island, and find their way into the woman's vagina when she is bathing in the sea. The woman nurtures the spirit, and gives it body. The man's role is to keep the baby-passage open with his penis, and lubricated, so the baby can come out. Because nobody needs to be assured of the paternity of children, women can be promiscuous. In fact, they are admired for it.

I went to the Trobriand Islands to see for myself if what's been written about the people there is true. It is. I asked them if they'd heard of ovum and sperm. They had, and they didn't care about them. As far as they're concerned, there is only one important word in the vocabulary of reproduction and that is *baloma*, spirit. The Trobrianders are matrilineal, which means they reckon descent, kinship, and all social relationships through the mother. All this is the complete opposite of the way our culture has developed.

People's theories about where babies come from are fundamental to the way men and women relate to each other. If we understand this, we're in a better position to understand other cultures around the world. And if we understand our own history, in terms of reproduction theory, we stand a better chance of understanding ourselves.

Anthropologists trek off to far flung corners of the world to examine the social patterns of so-called 'primitive' societies, but we need social anthropologists to examine our own society through the lens of reproduction theory. Our reproduction theory was, until the 20th century, as bizarre as that of the Trobrianders. We were 'primitive', just in another way.

Overall, European history of reproduction theory can be categorised as utter confusion. In 1685, the French physician Charles Drelincourt collected 262 incorrect theories of reproduction which, with his own, made 263. A hundred years later, the Swiss physiologist Jean Senebier wrote this:

"In vain a host of ingenious and profound men have assembled observations on this important matter; in vain the boldest genius has analysed this capital question. The passing of centuries results only in

a succession of errors, and whilst darkness the most profound has always obscured from the faculties of physiologists the secrets of generation, ideas the most incredible, contradictions the most flagrant, and travesties of nature the most incoherent have constituted the knowledge of those who flattered themselves on explaining the phenomena."

He sums it up nicely. Until the facts of life could be experimentally proved, misconceptions and arguments were bound to continue. The conflict only entrenched the male-seed orthodoxy, which could mock the confused scientists and point confidently to the Bible, which explained Creation to their satisfaction – with Eve being born out of Adam. For a scientist to suggest there are two seeds, that joined, and transformed into something completely new, was very radical because it contradicted certain Biblical concepts of Creation, and could even be seen as blasphemous. Furthermore, it smacked of occultism, which was a very dangerous route to take.

In the 17th and 18th centuries, scientists who thought along these lines were terrified they would suffer the same fate as Galilei Galileo who had, in 1633, been condemned by the church authorities for daring to suggest the earth orbits the sun. Galileo had to recant. To talk about reproduction was to talk about Creation, and God, and with the Church watching everything they did and said, it would have been reckless to suggest theories that were not within the male-seed orthodoxy and, in any case, couldn't be proved. As well as all this, and especially in the earlier historic period, most education was carried out in religious institutions and scientists were hardly likely to bite the hand that fed them.

Whatever scientists might have thought privately, they had to toe the religious line. They could do this quite easily by using the vocabulary of sexism. In the 16th century medical schools of Europe, for example, there was quite a lot of talk about female 'semen' but it was always described as 'ignoble', or 'lacking in copious spirit', or as 'useless and vitiated' – which means incomplete, imperfect, faulty, impaired or spoilt. Supposedly, only men were perfect enough to procreate. The word female 'semen' sounds positive, but the adjectives show that it was second-rate, and non-generative.

Reading old texts from the past, it's quite easy to misunderstand the meaning of a word by projecting onto it the meaning we have today. Many people have done this with Galen, the 2nd century AD anatomist. He used the word female 'seed' to describe a material he thought came from the ovaries. But Galen was quite clear that it "contributes nothing to the generation of offspring." We might understand the word 'seed' as an acorn that can grow into an oak tree, or as an ovum that carries DNA, but Galen thought female 'seed' was a sexual secretion that aided lubrication in intercourse, provided pleasure, and gave nutriment to a growing child. Same word, different meaning.

In the history of reproduction theory, two words might at first indicate that women were attributed a generative role, but on closer examination, they do not. These are 'ovism' and 'epigenesis'. The ovism story really begins with the events in Delft in the 1670's – when de Graaf discovered the Graafian follicles (mistakenly called the 'ovum') and, three years later, Leeuwenhoek discovered sperm. The scientific community was thrown into a frenzy of speculation. Some thought the (tiny) body of the child was completely in the 'ovum', and some thought it was in the sperm. These were the 'ovists' and 'spermists' respectively.

Spermists argued that as life starts with intercourse and semen emission, sperm delivers soul as well as body. Ovism, from a feminist perspective, was not as revolutionary as it first seems. First, there were many logical arguments against it, including the purely mechanical point that the contents of the ovary cannot, apparently, physically reach the womb. (We now know the ovum is released from the Graafian follicle, makes an heroic leap into the huge abdominal cavity, and is then captured by the fimbriae at the end of the fallopian tube.) Also, what they called the 'ovum' was actually the Graafian follicle, and it is too big to get down a fallopian tube, or through the sphincter muscle at the junction with the womb.

Moreover, although the ovist could speculate that within the 'ovum' there was a potential person waiting to get out, everyone knew that intercourse and the emission of semen had to happen first. As life only starts after this event, they had to assume that semen contributed something vital, if not the body itself. Ovism could thus imply that the ovum was a mini stillbirth unless touched by the mysterious "vital impulse" of men, which could be interpreted as life-force, soul or spirit – the difference between life, and non-life.

Both spermists and ovists were 'pre-formationists' – they thought the body of the child was pre-formed inside either the male, or female, body. The other way to think of reproduction was 'epigenesis', which essentially means there is a mixing of two materials from the male and the female. Aristotle and Galen were epigenisists, and neither of them attributed a generative role to the material they thought was contributed by the female. So, although the words 'epigenesis' and 'ovism' can, at first glance, give the impression that scientists were thinking positively about a female contribution, they were actually trying to work out how men reproduced. *That* was what they were arguing about.

All this is not to say that, in the long saga of reproduction theory, there weren't a few lone voices who were essentially on the right track. Leonardo da Vinci, for example, was four hundred years ahead of his time when he wrote the "seed of the female is as potent as that of the male in generation." He came to this conclusion after observing the dark skin of a child of an Ethiopian man and an Italian woman. But whatever the brilliant and eccentric Leonardo had to say, it was no help to women unless people in general believed him, and they did not.

Another person who was prepared to accept that women

played as much a part in reproduction as men, and who thought women were not inferior, was Epicurus, the ancient Greek who founded a school of philosophy in Athens in 316 BC, six years after Aristotle's death. The Epicurean doctrine of two seeds competed for a few centuries with the Aristotelian theory that men alone contributed seed – 'real' seed, that is. But Aristotle's theory was favoured by men, and repeated endlessly over the centuries as authoritative, while very few people ever got to hear about Epicurus.

The French mathematician and philosopher Rene Descartes, wrote in *Man, and a Treatise on the Formation of the Foetus* that male and female semen mixed, causing a "fermentation of particles." Descartes was trying to tie up his grand theory of mechanical principles and his thoughts on reproduction were the last piece in his philosophical jigsaw. The treatise was written just before his death in 1650, and published fourteen years later. And it was just as well he wasn't around to explain his thoughts because they were about as vague as a theory can get and, of course, couldn't be proved.

The next major scientist to propose a two-seed theory was the French scholar Pierre de Maupertuis, who wrote a paper called *Venus Physique* in 1745. He pointed out that astronomers and chemists had recently proved the law of attraction and asked "Why should not a cohesive force, if it exists in Nature, have a role in the formation of animal bodies?" He thought both men and women have "hereditary particles" in seminal fluid which, when mixed, results in a developing baby. His theory was strengthened when he met a family with extra fingers, and the inherited trait was transmitted by females as well as males. Maupertuis was radical for his time, so he published anonymously, waiting safely in the background to see how his peers would react. They said what he already knew – it was just unproven theory.

One of the first to experiment in reproduction was the Italian Lazzaro Spallanzani, famous for making pants for male frogs in 1784 and discovering that without semen, the eggs don't produce tadpoles. He also performed the first artificial insemination: he let one female dog be mounted by a spaniel dog, extracted the semen deposited in her and placed it in the vagina of another spaniel bitch – who produced three puppies some time later.

The mammalian ovum had not been discovered at this time so although Spallanzani was an 'ovist', and thought new life was pre-formed in an egg, and required semen – not sperm – to spark it into life, he couldn't prove it. He thought sperm were minuscule parasites, but he was surrounded by 'spermists' who thought new life was pre-formed in sperm. Human reproduction was still a mystery, and now a highly contentious one.

As time went on, more discoveries were being made in the fields of magnetism and chemistry, showing that materials can attract to each other and transform. So when Prevost and Dumas showed that frog eggs are fertilised by sperm in 1824, scientists were philosophically softened up to the idea that two seeds might transform into something new. A theory of life was forming – the 'new epigenesis' – but as Karl Ernst von Baer discovered three years later, the men of science were still not ready to accept the facts of life because of philosophical considerations.

All the men involved in the discovery of the facts of life had grown up in a world where it was accepted that men were superior intellectually, creatively, and in terms of their divinity. They thought they were profoundly different to women and, as it stated clearly in the Bible, biological inheritance was through the male line. Now they were standing on a precipice, observing a landscape in which all their preconceptions looked fuzzy. In fact they could see a new reality, and they weren't sure they liked it.

Creation comes with baggage – we know that because throughout the history of embryology men drew philosophical conclusions from biological facts. They extrapolated from the actual, to the philosophical, with the Bible as the backdrop. However, we know from anthropology that it's always been possible, just from looking at the very basic facts, to come to the conclusion there's reproductive equality. The two basic facts are these: males have a white liquid that they put in females; and females stop producing monthly red blood when they are carrying a child. This is the basic 'white-red' theory, of which many versions exist around the world and throughout history. What people said is that the white parts, from the man, contribute to the white parts of the child – the bones, teeth, brain, tendons, spinal cord, nails, whites of the eyes etc.; while the red makes up the blood and flesh etc.

This can be seen as a straight 50-50 contribution, interdependent, with no value given more to one than the other. But what happened in our cultural history is that more value was given to the white. In the 6th century BC, Pythagoras thought the soul and "moist vapour" from which an embryo would develop came from the brain and nerves of men, while women contributed the "grosser parts" – the blood and "humors" of the womb. The white brain, created from white semen, is seen as the seat of the soul – the essence of humanity, and alive-ness.

Every child that has ever lived, in every country of the world, asks 'where do I come from?' In the past they were given the wrong answer, yet that answer profoundly influenced their opinion of themselves, and their father, and mother, and their relationship with the opposite sex, and with their own children. And in many parts of the world today, children are still being misinformed, and misled into unequal ways of thinking.

SELECTED REFERENCES:
Senebier, Jean, in Spallanzani, M. L'Abbé, *Expériences pour servir à l'histoire de la génération des animaux et des plantes avec Une ébauche de l'histoire des etres organisés avant leur fécundation par Jean Senebier*, Geneva, 1785, page ii.
Needham, Joseph, *A History of Embryology*, Cambridge: Cambridge University Press, 1959.

Cole, Francis Joseph, *Early Theories of Sexual Generation*, Oxford: Clarendon Press, 1930

21: THE COVER-UP

Sexist men of science fought every step of the way to cover-up the reality of female reproductive equality. They came at the subject from a biased point of view and so their supposed scientific impartiality was absent. What they wanted to do was prove men to be the sole parents in terms of generation, seed – the source of life itself. To this end, they interpreted the facts the way it suited them and even ignored observations that weakened their case. Discovering the facts of life was not a straight, heroic march to the truth, but a prolonged detour by a bunch of guys who did not like what they saw on the horizon.

There weren't any women working in the field of embryology during the 19th century, and only a few working in cytology in the early 20th. That meant that publicising the radical, even revolutionary, discoveries about the role of the ovum in reproduction was left to men. And the funny thing is, the news never got out. It seemed to fall down a big black hole.

Bearing in mind the old truism 'the nature of power is to retain your power,' did men consciously, or subconsciously, take part in a sexist cover-up? Did they surreptitiously edit out from the new textbooks those elements of the story that drew attention to the fundamental change in the view of women's reproductive role? Whether conscious or subconscious, there was a silent conspiracy that left us with the impression that 'people have always known the facts of life.' Instead of highlighting the revolution, scientists quietly brushed their collective mistakes under the carpet and quickly turned their attention to genetics – a new science we could all admire them for.

Sexist editing had always been a regular feature of male culture, but 'the cover up' probably took more than that. Several factors converged to make invisible the shift that had taken place in the perception of women, particularly 'mother'. First, it was difficult to identify a specific time when 'the revolution' took place because it happened in so many small steps covering a century or more. Also, information had to come from the scientific community but during the 19th century there was a massive communication gap between the general public and the specialist scientists who were discussing the details of embryology in their private male clubs. No doubt too, the scientists knew the emerging 'facts of life' contradicted generations of eminent scientists who had gone before, and contradicted statements in The Bible ("he was still in the loins of his father" Heb.7:10) and, indeed, undermined men's elevated position in society. So they kept quiet. And women's liberation from incubator status became the most silent revolution of all time.

The twentieth century brought better education and mass communication but by that time the scientific establishment had assimilated the concept of the human egg and its fusion with sperm. Women's new role was no longer news.

Embryology involves sex and creation, which makes it open to theological, philosophical and sexual sensibilities. So of all the branches of science, it was more liable to be left out of discussions, whether at public talks, in drawing rooms, or in front of children. Somehow, the relevant books got pulled out of general circulation – put on the top shelf perhaps, and from there into obscure medical libraries under the heading 'the history of embryology', where nobody would see them.

Over the years we became less species-centric, and less reluctant to draw analogies between animal and human methods of reproduction. Indeed, we got so used to drawing conclusions about humans from research into insects, reptiles, other animals and garden peas, that by the time Shettles came along in 1960 and showed us pictures of actual human fertilisation and cell division, we were blasé. We hardly noticed.

22: DOES IT MATTER?

It's no minor incidental of history that we had the facts of life wrong – so wrong that men thought themselves the sole generators of life, and women their baby-making machines. Did it make men think they were superior? Certainly. And we know that because they said so.

Does it matter? Well, it matters to all the women around the world today who are still thought of as men's chattels – designed by 'nature' to be their property, and second class citizens. And it matters to the thousands of baby girls who are going to end up dead today, and tomorrow, and the day after. It matters to the women in sub-Saharan Africa who can't leave their abusive husbands because, if they do, they'll have to leave their children behind; the male-seed idea of parenthood binds women to men tighter than a ball and chain. It matters to widows in Nepal who'll never be able to marry again because men think their 'soil' is polluted. It matters to rape victims who can't tell anyone what's happened because if they do, no man will marry them. And it matters to children who are beaten, raped, and sold into slavery by men who think children are their grown seed, to do with as they wish.

The singular, male-seed, idea of reproduction led to all kinds of nastiness. It led inevitably to the major themes of patriarchy, and individual men put their own spin on it. Nobody stopped them because it was their right as fathers, progenitors, the source of life itself.

The traditions that grew up around the male-seed idea of reproduction made sense at the time, to women as well as men. But now we know the facts of life. What most people don't know, or speak about, or record in our history books, is the direct link between the male-seed idea, and patriarchal traditions. That's what we now need to talk about.

If we don't talk about it, tradition stays the same:	*If we talk about it, tradition can change:*
Singular, male-seed theory of reproduction = tradition of male supremacy. ↓	Singular, male-seed theory of reproduction = tradition of male supremacy. ↓
Nobody told about the male-seed theory. ↓	Everyone told about the male-seed theory. ↓
Think tradition of male supremacy was based on some acceptable logical reason (probably something to do with women having children and staying at home). ↓	Realise the tradition of male supremacy is based on old ignorant nonsense. ↓
Tradition stays the same.	*Tradition can change.*

23: PATRIARCHY UNDERSTOOD

Feminist libraries are catalogues of disaster, detailing the inequality between men and women, and describing the violence perpetrated by men, against women, to keep women 'in their place'. You can come away thinking men are naturally thugs and bullies, and women nincompoops to put up with them. It's all extremely depressing.

However, men had a logical reason to feel superior. It was wrong, but it seemed right at the time. That superiority was exclusive – it belonged to their gender alone. They thought it was 'natural,' which meant it had been initiated and intended by God.

The problem with the past is that it provides its own logic for the present: *it's always been that way*. We look at his-story and see men, men, men. Men running countries, fighting battles, conquering the seas and discovering new lands, creating great music, art, and philosophy, making scientific discoveries, and walking on the moon. And while men did all these things, women washed up. This scenario is so commonplace we think this is the basic, normal, natural, way to go about things and breaking out of this mind-set is difficult.

The average British working woman spends ten hours a week more than her partner on domestic chores. At ten o'clock at night she's sorting out the laundry while he watches the news. Whatever he says, it's clear he still thinks his time is more important, and that she's been put on earth to help him. Meanwhile, she's frustrated, resentful, and operating on daily low-level anger. She's probably fed up with asking him to do his share, and having rows. It's simpler for her to do it herself, angrily. And this is the thing – men and women are still engaged in 'the battle of the sexes,' to some degree or other, depending on where they live.

Scandinavia moved out of the patriarchal age decades ago, and the men share equally in childcare as well as in cooking, laundry and other household chores. Northern Europe truly lives in the 21st century and, coming from Britain, it's like arriving on another planet – a nice one. I once asked a Swedish man, whose house was spotless, "who cleans for you?" He looked at me, perplexed and irritated, and said "You think I'm a child and can't take care of myself?"

This is a very big world with countless attitudes, expectations and experiences. One of the most extreme differences is in the mental and physical liberation experienced by some, but not other, women. Likewise, some men are liberated from their mistaken sense of superiority, and others aren't. In the great scheme of things, we can expect that some countries will move into the equality position before others, some dawdle along, and others remain stubbornly fixated on the past. But change is inevitable. The male-seed theory of life was the mortar that held the tower of patriarchy together. That one, all pervading, idea made patriarchy almost unavoidable. But now, depending on where you live in the world, it's gone, or is in the process of going, or will go one day in the future. It's just a question of time.

Let's hope the women who are today subjugated around the world won't have to battle to win each and every freedom. British women have fought, and continue to fight, many battles – large and small, political and domestic. But we've come a long way since 1913 when Emily Davison threw herself under the king's horse racing in the Derby, in support of votes for women. She died, and many other women were jailed and force-fed, for the cause. Eventually, in 1918, women over 30 who owned property got the vote, and all women could vote from 1928. Women in America got the vote in 1920; in Switzerland it was 1971; in Kuwait 2005; and in 2015 women in Saudi Arabia were allowed to vote for the first time, but only in local municipal elections. But they couldn't drive themselves to the polling station because women in Saudi Arabia are not allowed to drive. Indeed, in September 2011 a women who dared to do so was sentenced by a court in Jeddah to ten lashes. The fight for freedom is still a painful business.

The number of female representatives in national parliaments is collated by the Inter-Parliamentary Union (www.ipu.org) and, at April 2017, out of 193 countries 4 had 0% female representation – including Qatar, and Yemen. At the other end of the scale were Rwanda, Bolivia, and Cuba, with 61.3%, 53.1%, and 48.9% of women respectively. The United States was 100th on the world list, with women comprising 19.3% of the House of Representatives, and 21% of the Senate.

Statistics, of course, can be misleading. Saudi Arabia was at position 97 with 19.9% of the Shura Council being female because in 2013 it was decreed that women should comprise one fifth of the Council. However, Saudi Arabia is an absolute monarchy and the Shura can only propose laws to the King and Cabinet, but not pass or enforce them. That is not real power.

In the world today there is so much that seems anachronistic, unfair, and just downright disgusting – especially in regard to the treatment of women. But if the old feminism was characterised by anger, the new feminism should be characterised by understanding. There was a reason things panned out the way they did. It was a big mistake, that's all.

Men are not, by definition of their gender, lazy thugs. It might look that way sometimes, but those men are just languishing in the past. Women can educate them, or leave them behind. We each make our choice as to whether we're going to waste our time living in the patriarchal era that has, actually, passed, or whether we're going to live in the fresh, new millennium.

SELECTED REFERENCES:
For women in parliaments see: http://www.ipu.org/wmn-e/classif.htm

PART TWO: THE WIDER HORIZON

24: THE WIDER HORIZON

We now know when 'the facts of life' were discovered – around the beginning of the 20th century. And we know what happened during the male-seed patriarchal era that preceded that discovery – the horrible subjugation of women. And we know that tradition still carries on today. The next question is "when did the male-seed idea of reproduction begin?" The first thing to say is that there were whole swathes of the globe where the male-seed idea, and resultant patriarchal culture, never existed. And there have been other places that didn't have male-seed patriarchal ideas until they were invaded and dominated by cultures that did – Australia, for example. So following back through time, past the ancient Greeks, we can see written and artefactual evidence of male-seed thinking gradually becoming less absolute, then operating concurrently with other ideas, and eventually tapering off around 3,000 BC. That might seem a long time ago but we have pertinent archaeological evidence going back 30,000 years and that indicates there were at least two other major theories, with women at their centre.

The patriarchal smog that has enveloped us for thousands of years makes it difficult to conceptualise a world in which men have not always controlled women. You don't have to look far to find a cartoon of a caveman dragging a woman around by her hair. We have projected our patriarchal his-story onto the ancient past and think male control of women has been the universal and perpetual experience. This is why anthropology is so useful to us at this point. It shows that men and women can relate in ways that are entirely different to the patriarchal pattern we have come to think of as 'normal.'

In Part Two, I present a short collection of anthropological and other scientific information that shows our standard ideas about the male-female relationship, preconceived because we've been culturally saturated in the patriarchal smog for so long, are wrong. They tell us nothing more than that we've been culturally conditioned. We can see from looking at the wider horizon that men and women can and do relate in a much more egalitarian way. It's important to do this before looking at the ancient past, which should not be approached with a closed, sexist, mind.

While anthropologists routinely ask contemporary societies about their kinship systems - which delves into the question "where do babies come from?" - archaeologists studying the past have no interest in reproduction theory. I've asked dozens of archaeologists "what reproduction theory did these people have?" and not one of them knew what I was talking about. They'd not even thought about it. Instead, they assume people have always known the facts of life, and use words like "female fertility" and "fecundity" as if those terms meant something. As we shall see, the word "fertility" can mean at least four profoundly different things, each of which has a massive impact on the respect given to women, and the way men and women relate to each other.

I asked one archaeologist about the figurines he'd unearthed in a particular valley in Pakistan. Like 90% of human figurines dug up from the ancient past, they were female. I was curious to know whether, as at other archaeological sites from around 4,000 BC, there was evidence of a female-centred religion. He got angry, stood up, and said "Oh, you're one of those goddess people, are you?" He was being hostile. "Look," he said "the women in that area today have the exact same complicated hairstyle as on the figurines." I was staggered. Was he saying that you can tell from a hairstyle what's going on inside a person's head?

Like so many other people, he thought 'men have always been men', and 'women have always been women' and, no doubt, that 'people have always known the facts of life.' Well, they only just about understood them in 1,900 AD so I very much doubt they knew them in 4,000 BC. The question remains, what did they think about reproduction theory in that valley? And how did it affect the way men and women related to each other, and how they worshipped?

For too long now, people in important influential professions have projected onto their 'logical' field of study a set of assumptions about the 'nature' of men and women, based entirely on his-story, and present traditions, formed from the negative impact of the sole, male, theories of reproduction in which their particular culture is embedded. Those professionals need to start thinking outside that box.

In fact, we all need to start looking away from patriarchal patterns of behaviour, and the acceptance of that behaviour as normal, and start thinking about how we're going to live in the future. This is a quantum leap. And it's difficult to do because not only can we not see our way through the patriarchal smog, we're dragged back into the patriarchal era by a form of gravity generated by millennia of patriarchal culture. Liberation only comes when the patriarchal past can be seen for what it is: a short term, geographically defined but much travelled cultural aberration.

25: ISLANDS IN THE SUN

After reading this passage in the 1929 book *The Sexual Life of Savages* by the anthropologist Bronislaw Malinowski, I went straight to the travel agent and booked my ticket to the Trobriand Islands:

"The idea that it is solely and exclusively the mother who builds up the child's body, the man in no way contributing to its formation, is the most important factor in the legal system of the Trobrianders. Their views on the process of procreation, coupled with certain mythological

and animistic beliefs, affirm, without doubt or reserve, that the child is of the same substance as its mother, and that between the father and the child there is no bond of physical union whatsoever."

This I had to see:

"We find the Trobriands a matrilineal society, in which descent, kinship, and every social relationship are legally reckoned through the mother only, and in which women have a considerable share in tribal life, even to the taking of a leading part in economic, ceremonial, and magical activities – a fact which very deeply influences all the customs of erotic life as well as the institution of marriage."

To get to the Trobriand Islands you go to Papua New Guinea, and catch a small plane going east. There are 14 islands in the Trobriand group, and most of them are tiny specs in the hugeness of the Pacific Ocean. The largest island is Kiriwina, which is about thirty miles long and between two and ten miles wide. When I went there in 1987 people were living in scattered villages, in houses built on short stilts. The walls were made of woven leaves and the roofs were thatched grass. Villages communicated with each other by means of a drum – a dug-out log. People tended their gardens, their few animals, and went fishing. They looked happy.

According to the Trobriand life-view, men have nothing to do with procreation other than, with the penis, keeping the vagina open and lubricated so the baby can come out. The testes are thought to be only an "ornamental appendage." When Malinowski asked what they were for, "a native aesthete" explained "...how ugly would a penis look without the testes." The testes serve "... to make it look proper."

Life is a joint venture between women and the spirits of dead ancestors. The theory goes like this: a person's soul or spirit does not die. It goes to one of the furthermost islands, Tuma, where it leads a constantly rejuvenating, happy existence among other spirits. At some point, the spirit desires to return to the physical world and, with the assistance of a controlling spirit, does so after leaping back in age and transforming itself into a small pre-formed infant. It then makes its way into the womb of a living woman, who is always from the same clan or sub-clan as the spirit-child. She will be the 'parent,' as Malinowski explains:

"That the mother contributes everything to the new being to be born of her is taken for granted by the natives, and forcibly expressed by them. 'The mother feeds the infant in her body. Then, when it comes out, she feeds it with her milk.' 'The mother makes the child out of her blood.' This attitude is also to be found embodied, in an even more telling way, in the rules governing descent, inheritance, succession in rank, chieftainship, hereditary offices, and magic – in every regulation, in fact, concerning transmission by kinship."

The spirit-baby enters the woman's body in one of two ways. Either it enters her vagina as she bathes in the sea – the *baloma*, the spirits, having floated into the bays from Tuma on bits of flotsam or leaves; or it enters from the head, dripping down to the abdomen in the form of spirit-blood. Whichever mode of entry a particular Trobriand Islander believes in, and there are several versions of each theme, the process has nothing whatever to do with men. Indeed, even a woman who has never been touched by a man can conceive if her vagina has been opened by some other means, as was the case with the mythical mother, Bolutukwa, who lost her virginity when the water dropping from a stalactite pierced her vagina as she slept beneath it.

As proof of their theory of reproduction, the Trobrianders offer two facts. First, unmarried girls who undoubtedly experience a great deal of intercourse do not usually have babies. Second, hideously ugly women, with whom no Trobriand man would dream of (or admit to) sleeping with, do become pregnant.

If a baby is unwanted, herbs are used to bring about an abortion. There is no moral censure because "To kill a spirit by black magic or accident is quite impossible; his end will always mean merely a new beginning." They do not think of it as death, just postponement and redirection because the baby-spirit cannot die, and will come again into a body ready to receive it.

A man is father in two senses: as we would know it – the man who stands in "intimate relation" to the mother; and the maternal uncle. The father who lives in the house with the mother and children is *tama*, the man you and I would think of as father ... the man who has a deep affection for the children – who cares for them, plays with them, and helps with schooling. But that man is also *kadagu*, father to his sister's children, who 'belong' to his village. He has a certain authority over the children, and can ask for their help, as well as give help to them. It is his job to impart tribal custom, and he becomes more important to them as time goes on.

Women move patrilocally in marriage – to the man's village, but as children belong to the same clan as the mother, her children really 'belong' to her village and should know its particular customs. Wherever a child may grow up, his or her 'own' village is the one where the mother grew up and where the *kadagu*, the maternal uncle, still lives.

How do the Trobrianders explain a physical resemblance between children and the man who "stands in intimate relation to the mother" given that they think there's no biological connection between *tama* and the child? When Malinowski asked the question he got a "stereotyped" answer:

" '*It coagulates the face of the child; for always he lies with her, they sit together*'. *The expression kuli, to coagulate, to mould, was used over and over again in the answers which I received ...*
One of my informants explained it to me more exactly, turning his open hands to me palm upwards: 'Put some soft mash (sesa) on it, and it will mould like the hand. In the same manner, the husband remains with the woman and the child is moulded.' Another man told me: 'Always we give food from our hand to the child to eat, we give fruit and dainties, we give betel nut. This makes the child as it is'. "

The Trobrianders have been told about ovum and sperm but don't care about them. They find the physical details irrelevant. So the man puts something, so the woman puts something. So what? The body still grows in the womb, and the child is still a *baloma*, transformed.

Everything here is the opposite of the patriarchal life-view. Because sex has nothing to do with making babies, it's very free. There are no derogatory terms like slut or nymphomaniac. If you say a girl is a virgin, that's an insult. I was told that the girl with the most boyfriends on the go at the same time is considered the belle of the village. Premarital lovemaking is done in the bushes or bachelor's house.

It goes without saying there's no preference for baby boys, and the idea of infanticide is abhorrent. Because the mother is the 'parent', children go with her in the case of divorce.

Because children are the spirits of ancestors, usually a maternal relative, the idea of telling a child off, or punishing them, is not only "foreign" but "distinctly repugnant":

"If the children make up their minds to do a certain thing, to go for a day's expedition, for instance, the grown-ups and even the chief himself, as I often observed, will not be able to stop them."

If a woman has a child in the husband's absence he won't assume she's been adulterous, and will cheerfully accept her child like any other. If a woman isn't happy at home she simply leaves and, naturally, takes the children with her. She moves her belongings to her mother's, or to a close maternal relative's and, if she wants, enjoys full sexual freedom.

Adultery is condemned, whether carried out by the woman or the man, only because it's emotionally upsetting for the spouse. However, according to Malinowski, divorce is simple and, as with so much Trobriand custom, involves the giving of a gift. In the case of a subsequent marriage, the latter husband gives a gift to the former, compensating him for the gift he gave the woman's parents earlier. It's not unusual for a person to be married three or four times in a lifetime.

Malinowski was struck by the friendly and equal nature of married life, noting that men were helpful with the children and domestic chores. The women joined in freely with conversation and jokes, working independently, "not with the air of a slave or a servant, but as one who manages her own department." If something needs doing, the wife asks the husband to do it. Although the husband is 'master' of the house in that the house belongs to him and it's in his village, the wife is, after her brother, the legal head of the family. The wife has her own possessions and she and her family make a major contribution to the food supply of the household. In all, her status is equal to his or, to put it another way, his status is equal to hers.

SELECTED REFERENCES:
Malinowski, Bronislaw, *The Sexual Life of Savages in North-Western Melanesia*, 3rd Ed., London: George Routledge and Sons, 1939, quotes from pages, in order: 3, 2-3, 144, 3, 146, 176, 45-46, and 15.

26: DEEP IN THE FOREST

Geneticists use mitochondrial DNA (mtDNA) haplogroup analysis to try and find out who, living today, are our oldest ancestors. This study takes them to Africa, and to people of diminutive stature generally called pygmies. Separated by a couple of thousand miles, across the Congo River basin, are two groups of pygmy peoples known collectively as the Western and Eastern pygmies. Their mtDNA is different, although both are ancient. If we are looking for how our ancient hunter-gatherer ancestors related to one another, these pygmies are a good place to start. And the interesting thing is, whether from east or west, they're peace-loving people who practice gender equality.

Among the western group of pygmies, a group called the Aka live in the southwestern part of the Central African Republic. Their men have become known as the most attentive fathers in the world because, according to Washington State University Professor of anthropology Barry Hewlett, they keep their infants within reach 47% of the time. There is no sharp division of labour between the genders – both men and women take care of children, both men and women hunt, both men and women cook, and both men and women decide when and where to move camp. Gender roles are flexible, co-operative, and interdependent.

The Mbuti pygmies belong to the eastern group, living in the Ituri rainforest in the north east of the Democratic Republic of the Congo. Anthropologists Colin Turnbull and Patrick Putnam spent, between them, fifty years living with this group of hunter-gatherers. Turnbull wrote:

"Childbearing in no way diminishes the mother's importance in Mbuti economic life. Since they are perfectly capable of giving birth to a child while on the hunt, then rejoining the hunt on the same morning, mothers see no reason why they should not continue to participate fully in all adult activities. For the first three days following childbirth only do they remain secluded in the dark shade of their hut, gradually introducing the infant to the light of the camp outside. They rarely stay away from the daily hunt longer than this, never in my records for more than a week. They may take the infant with them, slung at the side so that it has constant access to the breast, or they may leave it in the camp with one of the other mothers; in the larger camps there is nearly always one adult woman who stays behind for some reason, as well as some of the elders and children."

The Mbuti home is the forest, "which for them represents the supreme creative principle." Sometimes they address it as *eba* (father) but "most of the time they refer to it as *ema* (mother)." According to Turnbull:

"... both men and women see themselves as equal in all respects except the supremely vital one that, whereas the woman can (and on occasion does) do almost everything the male does, she can do one thing no male

can do: give birth to life ... the Mbuti associate womanhood with the life-giving principle and demonstrate this clearly in their rituals, formal and informal."

Elders are thought to be "endowed with special spiritual powers because of their proximity to death and the 'other world'." However, some seem to command more respect than others:

"(The female elder) has both authority and power. She may be a gentle, loving, and kindly old lady one moment, as many of the older women are, but in a flash she becomes pure power and is heeded by everyone. Ridicule is an important element in all conflict resolution; only the old women come out into the open, in the middle of the camp, and make explicit criticisms. Men may use the same central position, which commands attention, but only to grumble or complain and perhaps make minor and rather petty criticisms that are most likely to be ignored."

Youths of both sexes "indulge in premarital sex with enthusiasm and delight. They talk about it openly, with neither shame nor undue bravado ..." For girls, sexual life begins with the *elima*: "When a girl first 'sees the blood' and enters her *elima*, there is universal rejoicing because 'now she can become a mother'." She can now participate in the courtship that takes place around the *elima* house, and is a preparation for marriage.

Premarital pregnancy is not a worry because the Mbuti believe it can't happen if the partners "hold each other by the shoulders and not embrace fully." Naturally, Turnbull found this idea intriguing and consulted with Putnam, but they couldn't record one single case of premarital pregnancy nor could they find "even a hint of abortion being the explanation." Extramarital intercourse is likewise not forbidden because the same 'holding shoulders' position is used and so, according to the Mbuti, it can't result in pregnancy. When a couple are sure they're right for each other, they build a marriage hut, move in, and start going hunting together. The shoulder-holding during intercourse stops and "they *know* that children *will* be born."

Mbuti women are powerful and are not incapacitated by their ability to bear children. Turnbull writes "as a male I am aware that it is the men who feel, to some extent, incapacitated." However, Turnbull also tells us that there is no "sense of superordination or subordination" and that the Mbuti "work hard at emphasising the complementarity of the sexes." This "work" involves a ritual tug-of-war in which no side wins, and the *ekokomea* – a transvestite dance in which each gender dresses as the other and ridicules each other mercilessly. On domination, Turnbull writes: "If anything dominates, it is that prime quality of *interdependence*, in such sharp contrast to the *independence* our own society values so highly."

SELECTED REFERENCES:
Turnbull, Colin, 'Mbuti Womanhood' in Dahlberg, Frances (Ed.), *Woman the Gatherer*, New Haven: Yale University Press, 1981, quotes from pages, in order: 212-214, 206, 211, 209, 211, 214, and 219.

27: AN ALTERNATIVE LIFE-VIEW

Patriarchal ideas and laws accompanied military, economic, and cultural occupation in many parts of the world. Sometimes the indigenous culture got wiped out entirely. In other places, it's still possible to discern that a culture was once female-centred, and in some places that core respect of the female is still in place. The African country of Ghana is a case in point.

The Ashanti (or Asante) Empire, established in 1670, was a magnet for colonial takeover because it was very wealthy, being the source of huge deposits of gold and diamonds, among other assets. The Portuguese, Dutch, Danish, Germans, Swedish, and British all tried to gain control over the centuries, with the British winning that battle and calling their new colony The Gold Coast. On independence, the country became Ghana. The capital of the Ashanti Empire was Kusami, and few people understand the culture of contemporary Ashante as well as Dr. Peter Sarpong who retired as Archbishop of Kusami in 2008. He explains that inheritance through the female line that was characteristic of the old Empire lives on: there is "a general precedence of girls over boys in the estimation especially of Ashanti women."

Sarpong writes "In contrast to the mother-child bond which the Ashanti consider to be a biological one, the father-child tie is regarded as spiritual." The child is actually made up of three elements – the mother's blood; the *kra* or life principle which the Creator gives to a baby just before it's born – "a small indestructable part of the Creator," as Sarpong puts it; and the *sunsum*, the spiritual inheritance from the father which "is thought to mould the child's individual personality and character", and which links the child with the father's *ntoro* or "spirit washing" group. Men are thus drawn into the process of reproduction but, because the biological link is entirely between the mother and child, and because the matrilineal system is so strong, the father actually has little say in the bringing up of the child even though it's known by all to be 'his'. According to Sarpong:

"Jural rights over a child lie with its matrilineage members. But as it is believed that by reason of the spiritual bond, dissatisfaction on the part of its father could be fatal to his child, conflicts between him and the child's matrilineage members are kept to a minimum."

Sarpong explains why, among the Ashanti, "the value of girls is almost inestimable":

"In them the matrilineage puts the hope for its future existence. It depends upon them to provide suitable persons to take up offices and to strengthen the lineage. Whereas the boy is completely incapable of providing successors for his matrilineage, in the girl the lineage has potential males as well as further potential females."

The Ashanti are matrilineal agriculturalists. Women own and work the land – which gives them financial independence; names and property are inherited through the female line; and the birth of girls is especially welcomed. The Ashanti used to worship a goddess, Nyame, who at a later date became a male god. Nyame, the god, had to share his power with Asase Ya, the earth goddess who was 'queen mother' of the gods. This relationship was reflected in the Ashante king/queen-mother relationship, where the queen mother was the ultimate source of power. Likewise, although men used to be the 'front' of the society as warriors who fought the colonialists, women owned the land and wealth and were the primary parents of the children. Today, men are still 'the front' of society in being army generals and the majority of government ministers, but women still hold the power that goes with biological and material inheritance.

The concept of the *ntoro*, through which a child acquires its individual personality and character from its father, weaves the two parental families together. Because it's important an Ashanti child knows its *ntoro* group, pregnancies are kept identifiable by the practice of monogamy or serial monogamy. According to Sarpong, Ashanti men: "... know quite well that any ill-treatment of their wives will bring the weight of their matrilineage down upon them to demand either better treatment or divorce." The Ashanti illustrate an important point: there is nothing 'natural' about women being controlled by men or locked into unsatisfactory marriages.

SELECTED REFERENCES:
Rt. Rev. Dr. Peter Sarpong, *Girls' Nubility Rites In Ashanti,* Tema: Ghana Publishing Corporation, 1977, quotes from pages, in order: 8 (Note 16), 5, 5-6, 6, 8, and 7.

28: WOMAN THE HUNTER

There's a very widespread idea that only men can hunt because they're generally taller and have greater upper body strength than women. This idea is a bit ludicrous when you consider that the Mbuti pygmies discussed in *Deep in The Forest* above, who stand around four feet six inches tall (137 centimetres), can bring down elephant and buffalo. In Mbuti society everyone hunts – men and women, young and old.

There are different forms of hunting depending on the animals available and the terrain, and each culture has their own way of doing things. Aka pygmies, who live two thousand miles west of the Mbuti, across the Congo River basin, hunt as a group using nets, with both men and women playing the roles of beater – chasing the animal into the net, and butcher – jumping the animal and knifing it to death. Animals caught in this way include duiker, bongo, and sitatunga antelopes. Women take their infants with them on net hunts, placing the baby on the ground while she chases the animal and kills it. Aka women do not generally hunt monkeys with crossbows, or spear elephants and red river hogs. Both men and women set traps and snares for smaller animals such as mongoose and porcupine.

Because men and women have similar skills, their roles can easily be reversed. There is personal autonomy, and men do not tell women what to do. Anthropologists studying Aka society remark they've never seen an incidence of male violence towards a woman. Divorce is a simple matter of moving out of the shared house. Although the three positions of status are more often held by men, they're not positions of power so much as influence – which is exerted through knowledge, humour, persuasion, and hospitality. Aside from which, they usually got their positions because they're the sons of respected elderly women. Women have their own ways of exerting influence, and overall the Aka are considered one of the most egalitarian societies on earth.

Successful hunting is about using your eyes and ears, tracking and stalking, and communicating and cooperating as a group. These are things women can do as well as men. As we learn from various groups of pygmies, physical size is not the key to hunting success. Indeed, the greatest handicap to women's participation in the hunt is other people's prejudice against the idea. Of the Agta negritos (also known as the Aeta) living in north-east Luzon, an island in the Philippines, anthropologists Agnes Estioko-Griffin and Bion Griffin write:

"It is no accident that only in remote mountain regions do women hunt. Farmers place considerable pressure on Agta to conform to lowland customs. All lowlanders regard hunting as solely a male activity and ridicule participation by women."

Left to their own devices, Agta women will hunt wild pig and boar, monkeys and deer. They go armed with a bow and arrows or, if they prefer, a machete and a pack of dogs. According to the Griffins, "women not only hunt but appear to hunt frequently. Like men, some enjoy hunting more than others." Biology is not much of a handicap:

"Among the Agta, during late pregnancy and for the first few months of nursing, a woman will not hunt. In spite of the small size of each residential group, however, some females seem always to be around to hunt, although one or more may be temporarily withdrawn from the activity. Women with young children hunt less than teenagers and older women. On the occasion of brief hunts – part of one day – children are cared for by older siblings, by grandparents, and by other relatives. Occasionally a father will tend a child. Only infants are closely tied to mothers.
Girls start hunting shortly after puberty. Before then they are gaining forest knowledge but are not strong. Boys are no different ... As long as strength to travel and to carry game is retained, people hunt. Our best informant, a young grandmother, hunts several times a week."

One study has shown that 85% of the women hunt, and that when they hunt as a female group they have a 31% success rate, as opposed to the all-male success rate of 17%. However, when men and women hunt together, the success rate jumps to 41%.

Aside from hunting, there are other ways in which Agta women do not conform to the stereotypical patriarchally-controlled female: "Women are as vocal and as critical in reaching decisions as are men ... Agta women are actually more aggressive traders than are men, who do not like confrontation ... almost certainly girls are able to engage in sexual activity with relative ease"; and as far as extramarital sexual relations are concerned, "neither males nor females seem to be especially singled out for criticism – either sex may divorce the other with equal ease." Estioko-Griffin and Griffin conclude that "Agta women are equal to men."

SELECTED REFERENCES:
Hewlett, Barry S., *Intimate Fathers: The Nature and Context of Aka Pygmy Paternal Infant Care*, Ann Arbor: The University of Michigan Press, 1991, pages 23-42.
Estioko-Griffin, Agnes, and Griffin, P. Bion, 'Woman the Hunter: The Agta', in Dahlberg, Frances (Ed.), *Woman the Gatherer*, New Haven: Yale University Press, 1981, quotes from pages, in order, 143-4, 131, and 140.
Biesele, Megan, and Barclay, Steve, 'Ju/'Hoan Women's Tracking Knowledge and it's Contribution to Their Husbands' Hunting Success', African Study Monographs, Suppl.26: 67-84, March 2001, https://jambo.africa.kyoto-u.ac.jp/kiroku/asm_suppl/abstracts/pdf/ASM_s26/06_megan.pdf

29: WOMAN THE PROVIDER

For most of our existence on earth humans have been hunter-gatherers. There have been many different climatic conditions to deal with, at different times, and in different places. But, of the hunter-gatherer societies we know about, 70-80% of their food comes from gathering, which is generally done by women.

Gatherers must know the difference between nutritional

foods and poisonous ones. They need to recognise that under a few shrivelled leaves lying on the surface of the ground a tuber can be found. On a daily excursion a gatherer might find edible leaves, roots, stems, bulbs, fungi and honey. They will pick up extra protein in the form of eggs, insects, lizards and other small animals. If they live by water, they can fish, and by the sea they can gather molluscs and seaweed.

The Aka, who live in a lush plant-rich African forest, cannot gather all the thousands of plants they see around them. According to the anthropologist Barry Hewlett, their plant diet mostly comprises 8 species of roots, 11 types of leaves, 17 types of nut, 17 fruits, and 12 species of mushrooms. Of all the innumerable insects in the forest, the Aka only eat crickets, 4 species of termites, 3 grubs, and 12 caterpillars.

Gatherers need to be highly knowledgeable about their environment, and remember where the food sources are. And they need to communicate the positive or negative value of different species to their children. It was thus much more likely to have been gathering that developed human language, rather than hunting, which is of necessity a silent activity. Also, gatherers need containers to carry the booty home; and they need to devise equipment to hold an infant secure against their body while they work. Professor of Anthropology at the University of California, Adrienne Zihlman, points out that:

"… behaviours attributed to hunting can as easily be explained by gathering: long distance walking, use of tools, sharing resources, large home range, home base, low population density, detailed knowledge of the environment, and cognitive mapping."

Zihlman speculates that social groups developed around a female core:

"Sharing patterns established between mothers and offspring continued into adulthood and expanded to include other adult males and non-related individuals."

It's often said that men invented tools when they started hunting. People came to this conclusion before they considered the fact that tools used in gathering are biodegradable. We thought stone tools were the first simply because they preserved through time; unlike digging sticks, they had not turned to dust. However, as Zihlman points out:

"...wooden spears and, later, hafted tools, fishing nets and the like may have developed from digging sticks or 'bags' for collecting and carrying, in the same way that digging sticks may have emerged from an ape's termiting stick."

Also, stone tools were probably used for many thousands of years before people started hunting. The Kung San women of southern Africa carry a stone 'chopper' to sharpen their digging sticks, and Australian Aboriginals use organic tools which they make with stone tools. The first evidence of tools used in connection with meat may not indicate hunting, but butchering. The famous Olduvai Gorge finds in Tanzania, dated between 1.6 and 1.8 million years old, were discovered in an area that was once a swamp. The paleoanthropologist Mary Leakey suggested that the ancient hippo and elephants had become mired and, as Zihlman suggests, butchering such an animal "could as easily have been done by women with children as by men."

SELECTED REFERENCES:
Hewlett, Barry S., *Intimate Fathers: The Nature and Context of Aka Pygmy Paternal Infant Care*, Ann Arbor: The University of Michigan Press, 1991, page 23.
Zihlman, Adrienne, 'Women as Shapers of the Human Adaptation', in *Woman the Gatherer* (Ed. Frances Dahlberg, New Haven: Yale University Press, 1981, quotes from pages, in order, 108, 109, and 107.

30: CONTROL FREAKS

I've heard many justifications for male control over women. One man told me that men's control of women is naturally mirrored by the act of sexual intercourse in which the male must control the rhythm of the thrust. According to him, a man has to control sex because otherwise he would lose his erection, be unable to ejaculate, and there would be no children. I kid you not: there are people out there who think if men don't control women the human race will come to an end.

I didn't bother explaining to him that human sex can occur anywhere on a spectrum – with intercourse like animals in the field at one end of the spectrum, and Tantric sex at the other. In all aspects of human experience there are potentials, not absolutes. In terms of control, men are not only different from each other depending on the country and culture they come from, and the historical period they live in, but even on the same street in the same city two men can be a million miles apart. One man might be a gentle paediatrician and the other a controlling paedophile. You can't tell which is which from looking at their physiology. To understand control, you have to look into the mind.

The acceptance of 'controlling man' has a long history. In 1871, Charles Darwin wrote this:

"Man is more powerful in body and mind than women, and in the savage state he keeps her in a far more abject stage of bondage than does the male of any animal; therefore it is not surprising that he should have gained the power of selection."

Yet Darwin was aware that male animals have evolved all manner of devices to make themselves attractive to females and that, in most species, the female animal selects. He also knew of "utterly barbarous tribes" in which "the women have more power in choosing, rejecting, and tempting their lovers, or of afterwards changing their husbands, than might have been expected" – expected, that is, by the patriarchal 19th century male.

In the quest to justify male control of the female, men turn to animals, particularly our nearest animal relatives, the primates. But if you're going to extrapolate from the behaviour of monkeys, to arrive at an indication of what is 'natural' behaviour for males and females, which monkeys do you choose? – the baboon who lives on the savannah, or the baboon who lives in the jungle? They behave very differently. Studies in DNA and proteins show that the African chimpanzee is a 'sibling species' but as we diverged from a common ancestor at least five million years ago, we haven't now a great deal in common except our chromosomes. But, only because everyone else does it, let's talk monkeys.

SELECTED REFERENCES:
Darwin, Charles, *The Descent of Man, and Selection in Relation to Sex*, London: John Murray, 1871, various editions: Chapter 20.

31: MONKEY TALK

Ape society is hierarchical. We evolved from apes. We became hunter-gatherers. Hunter-gatherers are remarkably egalitarian. This distinct break with the social arrangement of apes is known as the 'egalitarian revolution'. In other words, things changed dramatically. Nevertheless, evolutionary anthropologists spend a lot of time comparing us to monkeys.

When they first started studying primates, researchers thought they'd reach neat conclusions about the 'natural' behaviour of primates and, by extension, humans. Then they realised that different primate species behave very differently. So they had to do more research, on more species, in more places, in more seasons. We've now reached a point where no group of monkeys in the wild is safe from primatologists who want to weigh them, measure them, take their DNA, and watch them eat, have sex, fight, groom, and pee. They even measure their testicles. So what does all this tell us?

Comparing different groups of chimps, researchers Johan

Lind and Patrik Lindenfors found that "Female chimpanzees use tools more frequently than males," and that females are the 'carriers' of chimp culture. Female chimps take care of the children, including finding food for them to eat. Male chimps generally only feed themselves, but when a hunt takes place they share meat with females, both in estrous (sexually receptive at the time), and anestrous (not sexually receptive at the time). Researchers Cristina Gomes and Christophe Boesch found with wild chimpanzees that "if a male shared meat with a particular female, his mating success on average was twice as large as if he did not share meat with the female." The sharing male chimp is a DNA winner. However, he doesn't know that because paternity isn't recognised. What he cares about is sex, and he's smart enough to know that if he gives a female food today, she'll let him have sex with her in the long-term, when she's in estrous, sometime in the future.

Working with a variety of primates, researchers have made the following findings. The central core of a primate group consists of several females and their offspring, including older 'boys'. The leading females decide when and where the troop move. Female primates stand up to males, form alliances against aggressive ones, and oust them from the troop. Female baboons form friendships with both males and females, but adult males don't have friends. Chimps hunt other monkeys in male and female groups, but the males make 92% of the kills by charging, throwing, and clubbing their prey.

There are two very different types of chimp: the murderous so called 'common' chimp, *Pan troglodytes*, and the altogether much more peaceful and sexy bonobo chimp, *Pan paniscus*. In a 2014 study published in *Nature* magazine, information was collated from 30 primatologists, covering 152 killings in 18 chimpanzee and 4 bonobo communities, observed over 5 decades. Of these killings, only 1 was suspected to have been carried out by the bonobo.

Scientists working on primate intelligence admire bonobos

because they're smart enough to understand abstract symbols and language. They can even count. Were it not for the fact that they can't make consonant sounds, we might be able to have an intelligent conversation with them. They certainly understand what we say. Although there's temporary male and female pair-bonding, the bonobos are a remarkably amorous lot, indulging in a great deal of erotic activity, male-female, male-male, and female-female. Bonobo society is centred around caring for the young, who take five years to wean, and female dominance in social groupings is greater than in other chimp species. That might account for the fact that bonobos make love, not war.

Geneticists are very keen to discover whether humans are closer to common chimps or bonobos, and a paper published in Nature magazine in 2012 started that process. It showed that, despite their profound social differences, the two species of chimps share 99.6% of their genome. We humans, meanwhile, share 98.7% of our genome with the bonobo. Further work needs to be done on our genetic primate heritage before it can be established whether we're closer to the common chimp or the bonobo. That will be interesting but, and here's the point, our lineage diverged from our evolutionary cousins 5 million years ago and we've moved on.

SELECTED REFERENCES:
Lind J, Lindenfors P (2010) 'The Number of Cultural Traits is Correlated with Female Group size but Not with Male Group Size in Chimpanzee Communities', PloS ONE 5(3): e9241.doi:10.1371/journal.pone.0009241
Gomes CM, Boesch C, (2009) 'Wild Chimpanzees Exchange Meat for Sex on a Long-Term Basis', PloS ONE 4(4): e5116. Dol:10.1371/journal.pone.0005116.
Wilson, Michael L., et al, Lethal aggression in Pan is better explained by adaptive strategies than human impacts, Nature, 513, 414-417, (18 September 2014).
Prüfer, Kay, et al, The bonobo genome compared with the chimpanzee and human genomes, Nature, 486, 527-531, (28 June 2012).

32: THE DENTAL RECORDS

Today, human males are larger than females to a ratio of about 100:84. The question is, are men bigger because, over time, the larger men pushed aside the smaller men in their rush to have sex with females? Did male aggression ensure their DNA got delivered, and give the thug an evolutionary advantage?

Aggression in mammals generally is accompanied by prominent canine teeth, so looking at the dental records of humans who lived many thousands of years ago is a way to determine if men were more aggressive than females. However, the records show there was no difference in their canine teeth, and anthropologist Adrienne Zilhman explains why this is significant:

"The fact that they are small and nondimorphic among early hominids could reflect greater sociability among individuals, between males and females, females and females, and a reduction of male-male competition and aggression ..."

Judging from other mammals, perhaps males got larger simply because they tend to feed themselves while females feed the children as well as themselves. Sharing made females smaller.

SELECTED REFERENCES:
Zihlman, Adrienne, 'Women as Shapers of the Human Adaptation', in *Woman the Gatherer* (Ed. Frances Dahlberg), New Haven: Yale University Press, 1981, page 102.

33: WOMEN: THE CIVILIZING FORCE

Precisely because women give birth, suckle babies at their breasts and care for their children over many years, women became the prime movers in socialisation and civilisation. We learned to speak while in mother's arms – not while out on the silent hunt. Mother taught us caring and sharing. She fed us, carried us around, protected us when we were in danger, and healed us when we were ill. Women developed social skills because they needed each other for communal childcare. The first tools were the digging sticks women used to gather enough food to feed the children, and the containers they devised to carry that food, and the slings they needed to carry the infants they held against their bodies as they worked. Women were the first horticulturists, and the first agriculturists. As archaeologist Margaret Ehrenberg explains:

"The crucial steps in human development were predominantly inspired by females. These included economic and technological innovations, and the role of females as the social centre of groups. This contrasts sharply with the traditional picture of the male as protector and hunter, bringing food back to the pair bonded female. That model treats masculine aggression as normal, assumes that long-term, one-to-one, male-female bonding was a primary development, with the male as the major food provider, and that male dominance was inherently linked to hunting skills. None of these patterns, however, accords with the behaviour of any but the traditional Western male. Other male primates do not follow this pattern, nor do non-Western human groups, in particular those foraging societies whose lifestyle in many ways accords most closely with putative early human and Paleolithic cultural patterns."

As a clue to the past, contemporary hunter-gatherers are interesting because they prove the point that there's nothing 'natural' about men controlling women. They also prove that women are not incapacitated by having children; that the nature of women's work was not limited by biology. Another important point is made by anthropologist Frances Dahlberg:

"Women among foragers participate in religious ceremonies and rituals; and the gods, mythical founders, and shamans are both male and female. Witches may be of either sex; they are not predominantly male, as is common in pastoral or agricultural societies."

Before men took credit for having the sole seed or spark of life, and took control over the means of reproduction, women, there was a whole other way of looking at things. We know this from the earliest written words. When we go much further back in time, to the wordless era, it gets very enigmatic. Understanding what was in people's heads is problematic, but less so when the patriarchal fog of prejudice is wiped away from the eyes. And what you see are images of females – a huge number of them, dating from about 35,000 years ago.

In 2008 a find was made at the Hohle Fels Cave in Germany. It's a typical Upper Paleolithic figurine, a 1.2 inch (6cm) high faceless woman with huge breasts and prominent genitalia. My local paper, the London *Metro* invited its readers to "Say hallo to the ancient equivalent of the Page 3 girl." For those who don't know, the "Page 3" girls are topless models displayed in tabloid newspapers for the titillation of their male readers. The *Metro* title their article "I've still got it at 35,000." *The Independent* newspaper takes a similar line with their "After 35,000 years, erotic art for cavemen discovered."

This interpretation of the female figurines as sex objects for men has been going on for a long time. In 1930, a French professor of philosophy, Luquet, wrote that they did not represent fertility, or the well-being of the social group, but the "voluptuous character" of women, saying the artist was imagining or remembering "his own sensual satisfactions." Archaeologists today don't talk in this overt sexist fashion, but they still refer to the figurines as "fertility figures," or "earth mothers," and there is still confinement in the vocabulary that reduces any female into the 'sex = fertility = mother' box.

But there is more to women than fertility and motherhood. As we shall see in Part Three, women once held professions and high offices that became closed to them when the male-seed patriarchal era took hold. It is very clear from the written record, and more so from the earlier visual record, that women were once afforded a degree of respect we couldn't even imagine for ourselves today. None of this makes sense until we ask "where did they think babies come from?" People did not think in terms of male seed when they weren't even aware of the power of seeds, and that only happened with the agricultural revolution that began around 10,000 BC, and then took thousands of years to spread. But before the idea that life started with a male seed, people had the idea that life developed from seeds inside women. Men were needed to water that seed, but women were the source and consequently seen as the parents. Seeds are singular – one seed gives rise to a plant laden with the seed of future generations. When people started thinking about seeds it was an either/or question: is the seed from the man, or inside the woman? People argued about that for millennia.

Every person who ever lived has asked the question – "where did I come from?" During the patriarchal era the answer was 'father'. Before patriarchy, the answer was "mother." And that period of time was very long indeed, making patriarchy a mere blip in the story of humankind.

SELECTED REFERENCES:
Ehrenberg, Margaret, *Women in Prehistory*, London: British Museum Publications, 1989, page 50.
Dahlberg, Frances, (Ed.), 'Introduction', in *Woman the Gatherer*, New Haven: Yale University Press, 1981, page 26.
Metro, London, 14th May 2009, page 7.
Connor, Steve, *The Independent*, London, 14th May 2009.
Luquet, Georges-Henri, *The Art and Religion of Fossil Man*, New Haven: Yale University Press, 1930, page 110.

PART THREE: HER STORY

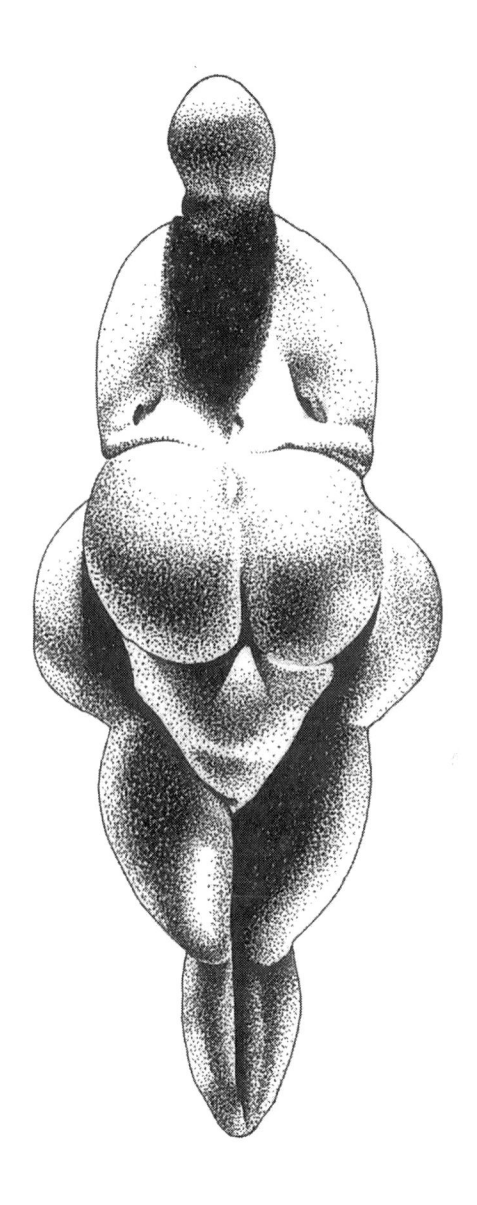

Fig. 2. Venus of Lespugue 23,000 BC. Mammoth ivory, 14.7cm high, Lespugue, France.

34: HER STORY

When Cleopatra was a little girl in the 1st century BC, the Greek writer Diodorus Siculus was just finishing his forty-volume history of the ancient world. Of Egypt, he wrote:

"...they have taken the general position that the father is the sole author of procreation and that the mother only supplies the fetus with nourishment and a place to live, and they call the trees which bear fruit 'male' and those which do not 'female', exactly the opposite to the Greek usage."

The Greeks, and most other ancient peoples, had come from a tradition in which people believed the mother was the sole parent. The Greeks held on very tight to this idea despite being bombarded with propaganda trying to persuade them that, on the contrary, the father was the parent. This battle of ideas had already been going on for centuries when the Greek writer, Aeschylus, produced a play called *Eumenides*, in 458 BC. Plays were a form of drama-propaganda, and were performed in the open air on big civic occasions, in front of large audiences.

Eumenides concerns the mythological drama of the family of King Agamemnon who commanded the fleet that set off to rescue Helen and destroyed the city of Troy around 1,194 BC. Agamemnon had been forced to sacrifice his daughter, Iphigenia, to appease the gods, confirm his command, and ensure a favourable wind. On his return, he's killed by his angry wife and she, in turn, is killed by their son, Orestes. The play concerns the trial of Orestes, who is defended against the charge of matricide – killing a mother, by the god Apollo, who says:

"The mother of what is called her child is not the parent,
But the nurse of the newly-sown embryo.
The one who mounts is the parent, whereas, she,
As a stranger for a stranger,
Preserves the young plant, if god does not harm it."

Apollo calls as his chief witness the goddess Athene, who has her own history. In the earliest phases of Greek mythology she was said to have been born fully formed from Lake Trionis. As time passed, and some people came to believe the male was the parent, the myth changed to the story that Athene was born from Zeus's head, after he'd swallowed her mother, Metis. In the play, Athene is made to say "For there was no mother who gave me birth; and … I am for the male and entirely on the father's side." On this evidence, Orestes is acquitted because there can be no charge of matricide if there is not, in fact, a mother.

But the Greek people were not prepared to accept the male-seed idea of reproduction so easily, and fifty years later another playwright, Euripides, thought he'd give it another go. He wrote *Orestes*, in which the boy once again explains why he was justified in killing his mother. He's speaking to his mother's father:

"My father begot me; your daughter gave me birth,
Being the field that received the seed from another;
For without a father no child would ever be born.
So I reasoned I ought to stand by the author of my being,
Rather than the woman who undertook to rear me."

This idea, that the father was "the author" of a child, and the mother just "the field that received the seed" was not easily accepted by people because they had other ideas, and had held them for thousands of years. It's those ideas we'll be looking at in this section of the book, as we go back in time and find it wasn't his-story, it was her-story.

35: UNCOVERING THE ANCIENT PAST

We know from the earliest written records that women had an authority at home, in the state, and spiritually, that they were to lose. The power that had been invested in the female eroded and eventually the male-seed theory of life came to dominate and, with it, the power of men – at home, in the state, and spiritually.

Reaching back in time to before the written word, we must turn to iconography and artefact to help us understand what people thought. And what's clear is that they were obsessed with woman's reproductive parts – her vulva, breasts, and protruding abdomen. Not only did people make figurines of women, small enough to carry around from place to place, they engraved or painted images of women, or symbols of her reproductive parts, into cave walls. Later, on Mediterranean islands, they created entire temples in the shape of woman's bodies, with entrances like vaginas, leading down a tunnel to an open space, like a womb.

Archaeologists have uncovered tens of thousands of prehistoric figurines in the shape of people, and the vast majority of them are female. The female figurines have been found just about everywhere from France in the west to Japan in the east, and date from 30,000 BC. When an archaeologist finds a pair of tiny feet in the ground, he or she knows that as they brush off the ancient earth they will most likely reveal a vulva and breasts. If they found a male it would be so unusual it would cause an archaeological sensation. This emphasis on the female body needs some explaining.

Reproduction theory helps to make sense of the enigmatic past. We can see two distinct periods of time. The earliest is when people were wandering around, gathering what they could, and hunting the animals they followed. In many places it was freezing cold. The images left to us from the period before 10,000 BC indicate people thought women reproduced parthenogenetically – on their own, without men.

When people discovered the power of seeds, everything changed. To begin with, they gathered wheat that had grown from seed that lay dormant in the ground, until the rain made it germinate and grow. When they looked for the source of human seed, they looked first to the woman. The baby emerged from her as plants emerge from the ground. But the seed in her needed watering – and that's when men came in. Men were the waterers.

This revolution in reproduction theory probably began around 10,000 BC in Ufra (now called Sanliurfa), in southern Turkey, near the border with Syria. Very slowly, over many thousands of years, this idea moved east and west, until it was the standard reproduction theory of the Neolithic age.

This was the state of play when the male-seed idea came along, more or less around the time of the invention of the plough, around 3,000 BC. But there were people thousands of years later than this who still refused to believe in the male-seed idea. And nobody could prove who was right, or wrong. But, because seeds are singular, this was an either/or debate. It was either inside the woman; or it came from the man and was planted in the woman.

One seed has the potential to create an entire tree, laden with fruit, and further generations of seed, or the potential to create an entire tribe of people. If women were the generants, the source of human seed and life, they would be the ancestors of old and the parents of the young, and they'd have spiritual and societal authority as a result. If men were the generants, they would be the ancestors and parents, and would have spiritual and societal authority. In the reproduction argument, there was a lot at stake.

The switch from female-centered to male-centered cultures was one of the most widespread and profound changes in human history. It seems to have been ignored or denied because many people find it too difficult to accept that women once had authority over men. This reluctance is understandable, given that we're so used to the notion that men have some kind of 'natural' authority over women. That's traditional, after all. But in a world where men were not recognized as fathers, where they played no part in the mystery of life, they would have no authority over women. Even in the female-seed era men were just helpers, facilitators, waterers of the seed. But women had the seed, and they were the parents ... the only parents. And that's what gave them authority.

Women having authority does not equate to women controlling men. A female-centred reproduction theory is not a mirror of a male-centred reproduction theory for one very simple reason. With the male seed theory the source of the seed, the man, is in a different physical body to the means of reproduction, the woman. To ensure he has control of his seed, he feels he has to control the woman. And when he thought the baby was either 100% his, or 100% some other man's, the degree of that control was extreme. However, with a reproduction theory in which the woman is the source of the seed, the seed both originates in her and grows in her. There's no need for her to control the man. She might want him to 'water' her seed, but there are plenty of other men out there who can take on that role. And before anyone had even discovered the power of seeds, and thought women were parthenogenetic, reproduced on their own, again, there was no need for women to control men.

36: WOMEN WHO REPRODUCE ON THEIR OWN

When I went to the Trobriand Islands in 1987 the people were living in houses constructed of woven leaves and thatched grass; now I see from Google Earth they live in houses with tin roofs. Times change. When I asked the Trobrianders about ovum and sperm, which they'd heard about, they told me they were physical irrelevances and babies grew from spirits of dead ancestors who had entered the women. Men's role was to keep the vagina open and lubricated so the baby could come *out*. Men, they insisted, had nothing to do with reproduction. And this is after a century of Christian missionaries trying to persuade them otherwise.

The idea that sexual intercourse has nothing directly to do with the production of babies was once extremely widespread, and has been recorded around the world by anthropologists since the 19th century. There have been many books written on this subject including *Primitive Paternity* by E. S. Hartland in 1909. He referred to early reports, from a time when many indigenous people had not yet been influenced by the ideas of the invading white man. In this two-volume work Hartland states his case for reproductive ignorance, and original mother-right, from all around the world. In his rather old-fashioned language he says:

"This past universality of motherright points to a very early origin. It must have taken rise in a condition of society ruder than any of which we have cognisance."

Throughout the continent of Australia, Aborigines from north, south, east, and west had similar ideas about reproduction, saying the spirit of the child came from some natural source – a rock, a plant, etc. – which came into the body of a woman, where it was grown. In a sense, even the mother is not a parent. The important thing is where the spirit child came from because that determines a person's totem-group. Men were required to be fathers – and the totem-group linked them to the child. Sex is just something pleasurable, unrelated in any direct way to conception. A comprehensive account of Aboriginal theories is found in Ashley Montague's *Coming Into Being Among The Australian Aborigines*, where he makes the important point that procreative beliefs are the starting point of family systems, social organisation, religion, and world view.

Every human being asks the universal question – 'where do I come from?' In the next section we'll look at the images left to us from 35,000 BC to 10,000 BC, to see what they tell us about the thoughts of our ancient ancestors. Before then, we need to ask 'was the female menstrual cycle the same then, as now?', and 'would they have recognised the connection between intercourse and, nine months later, the arrival of a baby?'

The numbers of menstruation, today, are 28 and 13: being 28 days of the menstrual cycle (not an exact number for all cycles but the number used by most doctors); and 13 being the number of cycles in a year. If you multiply 28 x 13 it comes to 364 – which is why menstruation provides a rough annual calendar.

In the Ignatievka cave in Russia there are paintings, dated around 6,000 BC, one of which shows a woman with open legs between which there are three lines of dots, totalling 28.

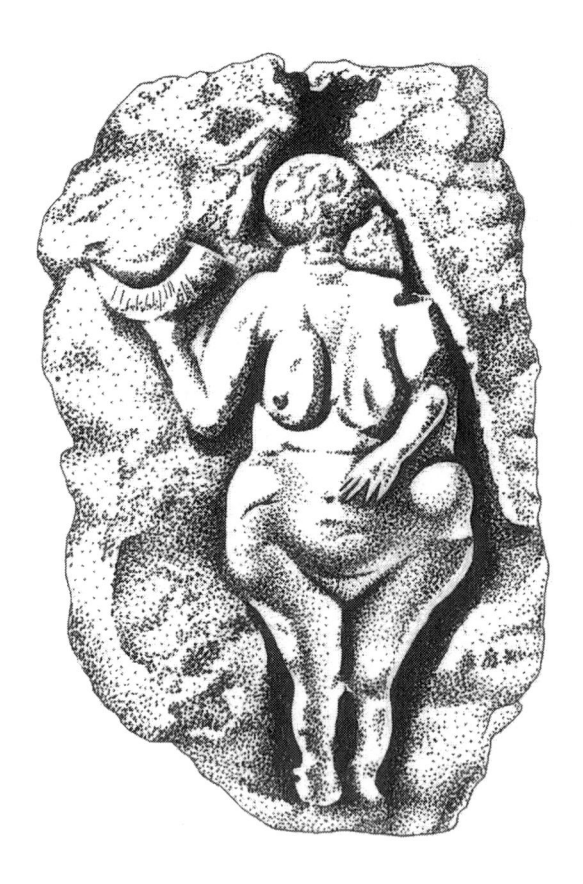

Fig. 3. Venus of Laussel 25-20,000 BC. Low-relief in limestone, rock shelter, France.

In the Dordogne region of France there's a low relief figure of a woman carved in limestone above the entrance to a rock shelter, dated between 25,000 and 20,000 BC. In her right hand she holds a horn with 13 incisions **(Fig. 3)**. Her left hand is placed on her abdomen. What message is she trying to convey? What is the significance of 13? Is this 19 inches (46cm) high figure known as 'The Venus of Laussel' proclaiming the significance of number 13 to women, and its relevance to the abdomen – to pregnancy and birth?

If these ancient images tell us that the menstrual cycle was probably always the same length as today, it also tells us that women ovulated, as they do today, for between two to five days a month. That means that then, as now, women could only conceive on between 26 and 65 days a year, and that intercourse on the other 339 to 300 days would not have produced a baby. For this reason, the connection between intercourse and babies would have been far from clear.

When a girl has her first menstrual period it is known as the menarche. To cultures all around the world it announces the fact that this female can now become a mother. However, the first bleed does not actually indicate sexual maturity because the hormones have not yet developed the internal organs so she can ovulate – which is the true test of sexual maturity. In a study by Dr D. Apter, 200 girls between the ages of 7 and 17 were measured at various time intervals for fourteen different hormones and steroids. It was found that, after menarche, there was a plateau for 1-2 years, before another surge of hormones and steroids took the girl to the point at which she was actually ovulating – and could therefore become pregnant. The study found that in the first year after menarche, 80% of girls were having menstrual cycles that were anovulatory (no ovulation); that by the third year after menarche 50% of cycles were anovulatory; and by the 6th year after menarche only 10% of cycles were anovulatory. In other words, although young women might have been having sex regularly after their first menstrual bleed, most would not have been getting pregnant.

Once women had babies, they would have breast fed for between 2-4 years – an activity that can suppress certain hormones and make conception less likely so, again, they might have been having regular sex and not become pregnant. Also, if the women were underweight due to lack of food, their fertility would be reduced.

Research indicates that only 13% of women living before 10,000 survived beyond the age of 31, and if that's so, nine months may have seemed a very long time, and the connection between intercourse and birth may have been hard to make. Also, a resemblance between a particular man and a particular child is less easy to see if that man's facial features are hidden behind a beard.

With all these factors taken into account, it's likely our ancient ancestors saw the miracle of life as an entirely female phenomenon. Where they had access to vegetation, they may have thought you pluck a baby from the body of a woman as you pluck a root from the earth, or a fruit from the tree. And if the ice descended on their landscape that would be the tradition they carried with them.

The concept of a woman who produces life without the aid of a man is very ancient and widespread. The Egyptian goddess, Nun, who was associated with the primeval ocean, created the sky god and the rest of the universe without a man. Similarly, the Sumerian goddess Nammu created the sky and the earth. The Babylonian goddess Dunnu founded the line, as did Danuna in Crete, Danu in Anatolia, Danae in Greece and Diana of the Gauls. While in Ghana the Akan goddess, Nyame, gave birth to the universe without a male, as did the Phoenician and Carthaginian goddess Tanit.

All these goddesses went through transformations, with their rank being downgraded as the centuries passed, as we shall see. However, at the beginning of their individual histories we hear echoes of a time when there was one spiritual source - a female, and one parent – the mother.

SELECTED REFERENCES:
Hartland, Edwin Sidney, *Primitive Paternity: the myth of the supernatural birth in relation to the history of the family*, (2 volumes), London: David Nutt, 1909, Vol. 1: page 257.
Montague, Ashley, *Coming into Being among the Australian Aborigines: a study of the procreative beliefs of the native tribes of Australia*, London: Routledge and Kegan Paul, 2nd edition, 1974, pages 389 and 230.
Apter, D, 'Serum Steroids and Pituitary Hormones in Female Puberty: A Partly Longitudinal Study', in *Clinical Endocrinology*, Volume 12, Issue 2, pages 107-120, February 1980.

37: MESSAGES FROM THE BIG FREEZE:
35,000 TO 10,000 BC

The earliest known drawn image of a human is of a woman's genital area, hips, and upper thighs tapering down to the ankles. Over 30,000 years ago, this 3 feet (91cm) high image was created using black pigment on a cone of limestone that hangs from the ceiling of the Chauvet cave in southern France. It has a very prominent position in the cave, being at eye level in The End Chamber – the last and deepest of the cave chambers, about 1,310 feet (400 meters) from the entrance. It was the earliest of the images created in this cave and its position makes it central to the activities that took place here.

Nearby there is a fissure in the wall: about 6 feet (2 meters) wide at the floor, 5 feet (1.5 meters) deep, and 5.5 feet (1.7 meters) high. The folds in the rock here make this alcove into a shape that resembles a large vulva. This natural feature is the central point of what is known as The Big Panel – a huge composition with a variety of about 30 animals appearing to both come out of the alcove, and enter it. Mostly they enter from the right, and exit from the left.

This concentration of animal activity around the shape of

the vulva is obviously quite deliberate because the opposite wall, which is smooth enough for similar decoration, has been left almost blank, except for 8 scattered animals, and a vulva drawn strategically above the entrance to another chamber.

Another fissure in this cave complex looks even more like a giant vulva and, again, it is the centre point of a large composition known as the Alcove of Lions in The Horse Sector. The recess is over 7 feet (2 meters) deep and around it have been drawn a large collection of animals including reindeer and horses, stretching over a 49 feet (15 meter) span. The composition emphasises the vulva shape and, in case we have not got the message about the importance of the vulva, a further 4 vulvas have been depicted on walls within the cave. There are, by comparison, no images of phalluses, or men.

The Chauvet cave is in an exceptionally good state of preservation because a rock fall 20,000 years ago closed the entrance to animals and people alike. Altogether there are 15 distinct chambers with 345 identified animals – 14 species, including lions, panther, rhinoceros, horses, bears, mammoths, reindeer, aurochs, ibex, red deer, bison, and musk oxen.

All caves have fissures through which rainwater percolates – usually just a dribble after passing through the ground above. Sometimes that water is red because it has passed through hematite – a form of iron oxide – in the ground above. When the fissure looks like a vulva, the hematite gives it the look of menstruation. This may have emphasised to ancient people the notion that caves were the inner parts of a great earth mother – the source of all life. This idea is confirmed by the fact that animals are depicted emerging from fissures and crevices at many other cave sites including Rouffignac, Clastres, Covalanas, Gargas, Niaux, and Janoye.

What was the meaning of this artwork? Some experts think ancient people saw the earth as the source of everything, all life. They'd watch the sun rise from the horizon, as if born from the distant earth, and then later disappear into it. Also, the moon appears to rise and fall into the earth. Even stars traverse the sky, and rainbows seem bedded in the earth. All plants emerge from the ground. Small animals burrow into the earth, and reappear from it with their newly born young. Birds fly off into the distant horizon, and come back months later. Ancient people would not have known that birds routinely migrate thousands of miles away. They just saw them come back, as if reborn. And although people followed herds of large animals on their migrations, at least part of the way, they would have seen other animals disappear over the horizon, into the distant earth. It may have seemed to them the birds and animals went into the earth, and reappeared from it. If so, the paintings of animals on the walls of caves deep inside the ground would likely have been an appeal to the earth to continue giving birth to all life.

The most famous art of this period are the so-called 'Venus' figurines – naked women, often with prominent vulvas and large breasts. They were called 'Venus' after the Roman goddess of love because early male archaeologists thought naked women inevitably equated with sex. Unfortunately, this is a theme that continues in the male mind, as we shall see.

In 2008, archaeologists found the oldest female figurine so far, the 35,000-year old Venus of Hohle Fels (also called The Venus of Schelklingen). This tiny 2.3 inch (6cm) figure was found buried 10 feet (3 meters) down in the ground of a cave in southern Germany. It is carved out of mammoth ivory and has enormous breasts, and a large well defined vulva. Her hands are resting under the breasts, on her upper abdomen. Instead of a head, there is a carved loop so the figurine can be worn as a pendant.

As a group, the female figurines of this period come from a vast geographical area stretching from southern France to south-eastern Russia, just north of Mongolia. These little sculptures of naked female bodies were made in bone, ivory, rock, limestone, and even, as long ago as 27,000 BC, in an early form of baked ceramic at Dolni Vestonice in the Czech Republic.

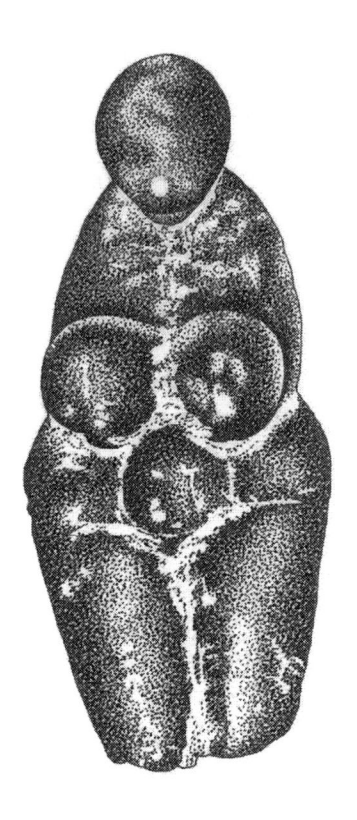

**Fig. 4. Venus of Menton 30-27,000 BC.
Soapstone figurine found on Mediterranean coast, France/Italy border.**

The figurines range in size but most are small enough to fit in a hand. They're remarkably similar in that they seldom have facial features – although the hair is often elaborately carved. Some are skinny and flat-chested, but most have large, pendulous breasts, a very pronounced vulva, and a great deal of body fat – especially around the buttocks. The figurines are not just about having babies – and in fact few are shown with babies – they are instead about the power that comes with womanhood – something inherent in the transformative nature of the person who is capable of creating life, whether she is now a maiden, a mother, or an old crone.

Fig. 5. Venus of Willendorf 30-27,000 BC.
Limestone figurine. Found near Krems, Austria.

The female figurines are usually known by the locations where they were found – and sometimes there were a few at each site. The places they have been found include: Avdeevo, Eliseevitchi, Mal'ta, Khotylevo, Kostenki, and Zaraysk in Russia; Gagarino, and Mezine in Ukraine; Dolni Vestonice, Jelisojevitchi, Pavlov and Petrkovice in the Czech Republic; Hradok and Moravany in Slovakia; Galgenberg and Willendorf in Austria; Hohle-Fels and Mainz-Linsenberg in Germany; Chiozza, Grimaldi Caves (Menton/Balzi Rossi), Parabita and Savignano in Italy; Abri Pataud, Angles-sur-Anglin, Brassempouy, Courbet, Enval, La Mouthe, Laugerie-Basse, Laussel, Lespugue, Mas-d'Azil, Monpazier, Pechialet, Sireuil, Terme Pialat, and Tursac in France.

The figurines often have pointed legs, without feet, and

could have been pushed into the ground to stand upright. They are small enough to have been carried from place to place and were no doubt among the most important objects people had. Sometimes they were made into pendants, and stylised, so we have another group of objects that look like an artistic shorthand of the female form (Petersfels; Engen; Neuchatel; Mauern; Pekarna; Mesine). This shape, the claviform, was also painted on cave walls, such as Chauvet, or engraved on cave walls including those at Les Combarelles, La Couze, Fontales, and Lalinde.

Vulvas were engraved or painted onto cave walls at La Ferrassie, Pergouset, Tuc d'Audoubert, Abri Blanchard, Abri Cellier, and Tito Bustillo. There are etched vulvas and breast-like stalactites on the ceiling decorated with red ochre dots at Le Combel at Pech Merle, and Le Portel. And at Pataud, a slim female looking just like a statuette – with head, breasts, torso, vulva, and tapering legs – was carved into the stone.

Images of the female form were also engraved in caves – particularly the abdomen and vulva – often using the natural curves of the walls, enhanced by engraving, to emphasise the female form. See for example: Les Tros Freres; Comarque; Termo-Pialet; Bedeilhac; the 3 women with pregnant abdomens etched onto the wall at La Marche; the 2 reclining women at La Magdeleine; the 3 women at Pech Merle; 3 abdomens and vulvas at Angles-sur-l'Anglin.

By comparison, there is only one location where a natural phallic-shaped stalagmite has been emphasised with a rough head and shoulder line, indicting a man (Portel). This just highlights the lack of interest in the phallic male in the spiritual environment of caves because they're all full of stalagmites that could have been decorated in this way. The fact that they have not been sends its own message.

At the Laussel rock shelter in France, a series of deep engravings known as low-relief were found. Four were of women anatomically complete, from head to toe: one holds a horn, another seems to be holding a stone lamp, another has an elaborate hairstyle, and a fourth appears to be kneeling on the ground, giving birth.

Most cave art we know about is located in France and Spain. The caves usually go deep into the ground and have a series of passages and open areas. The images are often difficult to reach, involving crawling through narrow passages. This artwork was not decorative wallpaper; it was ritualistic – it had a purpose.

The very impressive and widespread images of females have, since the beginning of Paleolithic archaeological research, often been interpreted by male archaeologists as expressions of male sexual fantasies. For example, in 1930 G.H. Luquet said they were about the artist's (he assumed to be male) "sensual satisfactions" (page 110). In 2005 Dale Guthrie wrote that the nudity of the female images indicated they were made by men (page 350). And in 2003, Jean Clottes suggested (page 202) that the area in which the 3 foot high Chauvet vulva was found might be closed to women (and children) and only available to initiates, who he assumed to be male. These kind of comments are part of widespread (male) notions of man-the-artist, and man-the-prehistoric-porn-maker.

I suggest an alternative view: that people who produced this art thought in terms of female abundance. That is, they venerated the earth as the source of all life, and venerated women for their ability to create life. And, crucially, it was a creative process that occurred without the male.

To support this view, there is the rather remarkable fact that images of intercourse are extremely rare. The renowned archaeologist Andre Leroi-Gourhan wrote in 1968 (page 482) that he knew of no certain images of sexual intercourse. And no new image has been discovered since to conflict with his opinion.

When looking at the earliest artwork produced by human beings, it is important to refer to photographs, rather than black and white line drawings. I say this because I have seen many drawings, supposedly copied from the original cave walls or stone plaques, which are not the same as the image in the photo. Indeed, the more photos and drawings of any one image that can be found, the less exact the drawings are seen to be. In other words, people project onto the image what they want to see, rather than what is actually there. This leads to all kinds of problems with regard to interpretation.

One much discussed image is the low-relief at Laussel variously described as a woman looking at her reflection in the water, as a couple making love in the oceanic position – facing each other, or a woman giving birth. If you have access to a clear photo you can see that the woman above is deeply incised around her head, breasts, abdomen, and arms, and is kneeling on the ground, giving birth to a baby – the smaller, lightly incised figure below, with head and shoulders emerging from between her legs. This is one image the 'intercourse-hunters' refer to as sex, but it is far more likely to be about birth – and reproduction.

Another image said to be of intercourse is at Les Combarelles. The line drawing made many decades ago by Breuil, and often used to illustrate the figures, is simply wrong, and an analysis of the photographed lines can be found in Leroi-Gourhan page 523. Basically, two animals – probably horses – and a few lines have been incorrectly copied to make it look like a human sex scene. It is not.

One image that is certainly a sex scene is found at Los Casares in Spain. On the right is a figure that resembles a dog, with a huge phallus, and on the left a figure that resembles a bird. This looks like inter-species animal sex, not human sex.

At La Marche, several artworks comprise a mass of engraved lines, superimposed upon each other until nothing is clearly legible. Few people have seen the original stone, yet many want to interpret the complex confusion of lines. The result is that we have a number of drawings, each different from the other. It is possible that out of this complex mass of squiggling lines a phallus and a pair of figures can be found, standing having sex. But no picture shows the figure on the left is female – it is just assumed to be.

These four images are the best we have from 25,000 years of artistic history that supposedly show sexual intercourse. It's not much. The 'intercourse-hunters' do put forward a few even more unlikely possibilities, and my advice is look at the photos of the original piece and then make your own judgement.

This lack of interest in human sexual intercourse tells us that it did not have significance to these people in terms of the big question "where did I come from?" Animal intercourse is likewise as rare. If people thought males were involved in reproduction there is no sign of in the visual messages they left behind.

Representations of men in art of this time are rare. Let me re-phrase that: images of men clearly shown as human, with a beard and/or phallus are rare. What has happened in this field of study is that any indistinct shape that might be interpreted as a human is automatically called "a male." There are only a handful of human faces shown with beards – apparently men in the ice age shaved: practically all the faces we see are clean-shaven. So any human figure that does not have a penis could, in theory, be male or female. However, if they have no sexual characteristics, they are always classified as 'male'. This is the case with particular examples from: Eyzies; Gabillou; Levanzo; Los Casares; Mas-d'Azil; Pech Merle; Raymonden; Saint-Marcel; La Vache; and Villars.

Figures are also called "male" or "sorcerer" (implied male) when they look entirely like animals (Chauvet). Sometimes these animal figures have human-like feet so can be interpreted as shamans – people who have special powers to perform magic and communicate with spirits, particularly those of animals. These shaman-like figures are assumed to be male even when they don't have a phallus, but do have horns, an animal head (taken to be a mask), fur, and/or a tail. Examples are found at: Abri Murat; Combarelles; Cougnac; Gabillou; Hornos de la Pena; Madeleine; Teyjat; and Villars. The tendency of archaeologists to jump to the conclusion that images of shamans inevitably represent males conflicts with the archaeological record and, indeed, contemporary anthropological evidence, as shown in HUNTING MAGIC, below.

The few figures that do have a phallus and look both male and shamanic can be found at: Gabillou; Lourdes; Roc-de-Sers; Trois Freres; and Tuc-d'Audoubert. And a group of figures that look like human males, but have animal-like or bird-like heads have been found at: Combarelles; Lascaux; Madeleine; Mas-d-Azil; Pergouset; and Addura. A mammoth ivory figurine found at Hohlenstein-Stadel in Germany, referred to as 'the lion man', has been reassembled several times from 300 tiny fragments so whether it was a man in lion's clothing, or just a lion, has been contested (E. Schmid 1988 and McDermott 1985). In any event it's impressive, being 40,000 years old and 11.7 inches (29.6cm) high.

Most images of men, or animal-men, or indistinct blobs assumed to be men, relate to the hunt. We see these often roughly engraved or unclear figures knocked down to the ground by animals, being chased by them, or successful in the hunt. Many of the images were engraved on animal bone or antler.

Leroi-Gourhan noted (page 482) that in the art of this time there are only about 15 representations of males with a phallus, including decorated objects, statuettes, and cave art. This is profoundly different to images of women which almost always show their reproductive parts – vulvas, abdomens and breasts – and, indeed, very often that is all that's represented. If these people thought life emanated from a female earth, and from female women alone, this is exactly what we would expect to see.

While over 120 female figurines from this deeply ancient

time have been uncovered, only one male statuette has been found – known as the Brno 'puppet'. This huge disparity in the number of females relative to males is also evident in cave art. Despite the glaring facts in front of them, many male archaeologists still over-play the existence of male representations. For this reason, in the next paragraph I'm going to describe every known example of male imagery, by location in alphabetical order. This will be very boring and unnecessary for many, and I apologise for that, but for those people who study these things I think it's worth getting specific.

At Bedeilhac there is a man seated, engraved in stone. At Brassempouy an ivory statuette may show a man from chest to ankles. At Brno, a male figure carved from mammoth ivory, thought to be a puppet or doll, was found in a grave of a male, thought to be a shaman. At Gourdan a male was engraved in bone. At Isturitz there is a 2¾ inch (7cm) stone engraving of a man. At Laugerie-Basse a bone engraving shows a man crawling behind an animal; and on another piece, 2 figures are shown fishing – one of whom has a phallus. At Laussel there is a low-relief engraving of a freakish man with a phallus that reaches from the ground to his waist; and another of a figure from neck to legs which has no phallus or breasts is categorised male but some experts believe it to be a young woman (Duhard, 1993). At Lourdes there is an engraving of a bearded man, with horns and a tail. And at Madeleine a man with a spear is engraved on bone; and an engraving shows a bearded man with a boy. At Mas d'Azil a bone is engraved with a man climbing. At Ribeira de Piscos a man wearing a head-dress, possibly horns, is shown ejaculating. At Saint Cirq a wall engraving shows a man leaning backwards – although he shows no sign of shamanic tools, he has been elevated to "sorcerer" status in many references. At Sous-Grand-Lac a tall man is engraved with his arms outstretched. Plus at Addura a group of people, male and female, are seen butchering an animal and carrying bags away.

There is nothing in the art to indicate that men were thought to play a role in reproduction. Men were most often shown in the drama of hunting, and most of the images of men are engraved on animal bones and antlers – trophies of the hunt. If masculinity was defined in terms of hunting, then we should also expect the penis – the male symbol – to appear on hunting tools. The phallus may have represented the power of men to overcome the wild beast. And that, in turn, may have become representative of sexual virility. Indeed, success in the hunt may have translated into success with acquiring access to sex with women. And sex is itself a powerful human experience and can be represented by the phallus without any reference to reproduction.

So it is no surprise that there should be images of the phallus itself. Phallic shaped objects were carved from animal horn and bone (for example: Mas d'Azil; Abri Blanchard), and in a few places were engraved into stone (Laugerie-Haute; Laussel). Another group of objects that were engraved to look like a phallus are the pierced batons made from antler or bone (Gorges d'Enfer). Objects like this are used by known hunting groups to give extra force to the action of throwing a spear, and experimental archaeology has shown they increase the distance thrown by between 43% and 127%.

The oldest 'phallus' is also from the Hohle Fels cave, and is 7,000 years younger than the female figurine found at the same site. The archaeologist Professor Nicholas Conrad has been reported as suggesting that this long stone was smoothed to be used as a sex aid. It may also have been made smooth by laying for years at the bottom of the river that runs nearby. It has an unusual long shape for a stone, inviting the comparison with a penis, which has been accentuated by rings engraved at one end. But, examination has shown it has scars typical of making flints, so again we see a tool used in hunting – to make flints for the kill – associated with a phallus.

There are remarkably few places where engravings of a

phallic shape and a vulva shape are shown close together, and they are never shown joined in intercourse. This disinterest in the visual joining of male and female sex organs is surprising, given that sex has always been humanity's number one pleasure. More sex graffiti can be found in any one youth club toilet stall today than can be found in 25,000 years of art from around the world, prior to 10,000 BC. Sex was not their obsession. But female reproduction was.

The ritualistic nature of art from this period tells us that the nomadic ice-age hunters were spiritual beings. This isn't surprising: spirituality is as old as people are – where you have people, you have spirituality. And even at this ancient time in history people buried their dead with care, putting into the grave things they might need in the afterlife. Looking at artefacts made at this time, the power of the female images are overwhelming. This raises a question people have been arguing about since the first 'Venus figurines' were found – what do they mean?

SELECTED REFERENCES:
Clottes, Jean (Ed.), *Return to Chauvet Cave*, London: Thames and Hudson, 2003, illustrations 102, 109, 126, 131, 165-8.
Leroi-Gourhan, Andre, *The Art of Prehistoric Man in Western Europe*, London: Thames and Hudson, 1968.
Graziosi, Paolo, *Palaeolithic Art*, London: Faber and Faber, 1960.
Duhard, Jean-Pierre, *Realisme de l'Image Feminine Paleolithique*, Paris: CNRS Editions, 1993.
Duhard, Jean-Pierre, *Realisme de l'Image Masculine Paleolithique*, Paris: Jerome Millon, 1996.
Wescott, David (Ed.), *Primitive Technology II: A Book of Earth Skills*, Layton, Utah: Gibbs Smith, 2001.

38: IMAGES OF THE ICE AGE FEMALE: SEX OBJECT? FERTILITY CHARM? CREATRIX?

It's amazing that *anything* can be found from 35,000 to 10,000 BC, yet archaeologists have uncovered over 120 female statuettes. Thirty were found at one site alone – at Mal'ta in the central Siberian plateau, and another cache of 11 were found at Gagarino, on the bank of the river Don, both in Russia. Although many female statuettes feature prominent vulvas and breasts, some represent slim women. Charming examples are the 3 inches (7.2cm) high dancing woman carved from green serpentine stone, dated 30,000 BC, found in Galgenberg, Austria, and the 5 inch (15.3cm) Yeliseyevichi figurine carved from mammoth tusk, dated around 13,500 BC, found in the far west of Russia.

The female was clearly central to the lives of people living in a vast area, stretching from Russia in the east to Spain in the west. By comparison, there is only 1 statuette that all experts agree is male: the Brno 'puppet' found in a shaman's grave in the Czech Republic. The only other contender is from Brassempouy in France: a figure from chest to legs with a lump that could well be a phallus, although some experts think it's an unfinished female. The site is famous for several female figurines, as well as a tiny mammoth ivory female head with a carved nose and brow, making it highly unusual because during this period the faces were left undefined.

Because archaeologists have talked for so long about the naked female images being about sex – male fantasies of sex, the media have repeated that idea. So, for example, we find that most prestigious international academic journal, *Nature*, filing a video on the Hohle Fels figurine under 'prehistoric pinup'. And when the film maker Werner Herzog directed a film about the Chauvet cave, he referred to the painted vulva as being part of a tradition that led to 'Baywatch' – the TV series featuring busty female life-guards running on the beach in slow-motion.

Some say the Venus figurines were not made by men, but by women who were concerned about 'fertility'. This 'fertility' is interpreted as desire for a child, or help during the dangerous process of giving birth. The assumption is that women made the figurines, carried them, and wore them as amulets. Partly, this idea developed from the fact that many figurines are found in places where people lived. But, of course, it was not only women who were 'at home' by the fire. Men were there too.

And if the figurines are about having babies, why are they not shown holding a child or giving birth to it? Or, why do we not see figurines of fat, healthy babies? And if the figurines are some kind of obstetric amulet, are they images of female ancestors who knew about the dangers of childbirth and how to avoid them? If so, why do they need to be shown naked in sub-zero temperatures? And why are they faceless?

The words 'fertility' and 'fecundity' are unhelpful because they can mean so many different things. To us, female 'fertility' is about ovulation and the health of ova; male 'fertility' is about the health and motility of a man's sperm. In the male-seed era, female 'fertility' referred to the quality of her 'soil' being able or unable to grow male seed, which they associated with ejaculate. In the female seed era, 'fertility' meant a woman having lots of seeds in her body, which would grow only if a man watered them. In the pre-seed era, female 'fertility' probably meant a woman being able to produce a child, without a man. Also, the words 'sex' and 'reproduction' do not mean the same thing to all people. Yet, because reproduction theory is not being discussed in archaeology, the words 'sex', 'fertility,' 'fecundity' and 'reproduction' are used interchangeably, as if they mean pretty much the same thing. To get anywhere near understanding the meaning of the female figurines we need to be more precise in our use of language.

The use of fissures in caves, the emphasis on the female reproductive parts, the lack of interest in intercourse, and in the male figure in general, point clearly to 'reproduction' being the subject of interest, not 'sex'. And that reproduction was apparently thought to be accomplished by the female alone. This would explain the tremendous emphasis on the female form – the body that can create life.

"Where do we come from?" is the universal question every culture asks. It leads almost inevitably to an outside being – a deity, ancestral spirits, nature spirits, for example. Next to this question about us, humans, is the question "where does all other life come from?" – plants and animals, because our survival depends on their birth and rebirth. Without them, we starve.

Today, even people with few material possessions will treasure some symbol of their spiritual beliefs. The poorest Indian will have a shrine in his or her home; while Brazilians living in shanty towns will have a crucifix on their wall, or around their neck; and Jews wear the Star of David as a pendant, or have a menorah – the seven-armed candlestick – in their home. These are the images we gather strength from. On spiritual symbols we focus our hopes, fears and devotion. Symbols are empowered, and empowering. They are our insurance and our escape. They're important and, probably, some of the first things we made. And what did we make? Images of women that were small enough to be taken with us from place to place. Often they were made with a hole so they could be worn as a pendant.

When asking why female figurines were produced on such a huge scale, the 'woman only' theories (about having babies), like the 'men only' theories (about pornography for men), are all part of a sexism that refuses to contemplate the idea that people ever could venerate the female. And it says more about the legacy of patriarchy than it does about people who lived 35,000 years ago. All societies have a spiritual system that crosses all genders – men and women think and believe the same thing. Why assume these societies were different?

If Paleolithic people believed that women produce children without men, after the onset of menstruation, there's only one thing (possibly) standing in the way of the baby coming out of the vagina: the hymen. This brings us to a question: did ancient people make objects specifically designed to break the hymen of virgins? We have to ask this because some of the objects dug up from the past look as if they could have been used for precisely that.

The Savignano figurine, for example, found in northern Italy and dated between 23,000-18,000 BC, was carved in serpentine stone and is 23cm long. The body is in the form of a classic female figurine of the period, but the head looks like a well-crafted penis. If this was intended as a tool of ritual defloration it would make sense to incorporate into the design a penis which is, after all, what goes into a vagina on a regular basis. And having the female shape incorporated into it could, perhaps, have signified the young girl's transition into potential motherhood – the female part of the object representing the initiate's own new ability to give birth. Or perhaps the female form represented the earth goddess – she who brought all life into the world.

The ritual breaking of the hymen is not, in itself, and unusual practice – historically and anthropologically speaking, and it is often the older women who carry out the task. The Trobriand Islanders of Melanesia think the foetus is an ancestral spirit growing inside the woman's body. The role of men is to keep the baby passage (the vagina) open and lubricated so the baby can come *out*. The Trobriand creation myths tell how the original mothers of the different islands had their hymens broken, in one case by falling rain, and in another by water dropping from a stalactite in a cave: "The drops of water pierce her vagina, and thus deprive her of her virginity." This was discovered by the anthropologist Bronislaw Malinowski, whose conversations with the Trobrianders led to the subject of the methods a woman might use to lose her hymen:

"In other myths of creation the means of piercing the hymen are not mentioned, but it is often explicitly stated that the ancestress was without a man, and could, therefore, have no sexual intercourse. When asked in so many words how it was that they bore children without a man, the natives would mention, more or less coarsely or jestingly, some means of perforation which they could easily have used, and it was clear that no more was necessary."

The ancient female figurines may have represented female relatives long dead, from whom the tribes originated – their first ancestresses. Males were not represented in the same way so that indicates they thought women were parthenogenetic and reproduced without men.

Alternatively, the figurines may have been part of the wider visual imagery we have from this ancient period, in which the feminine features strongly in cave art, in the belly of the earth. If so, the figurines may have represented an earth mother, a creatrix who gave life to everything – people, animals, plants, the sun and moon. Women would have been seen as her agents on earth, creating life and giving birth to humans from their vulvas.

Archaeologists find it controversial to suggest that the huge collection of female imagery from ancient prehistory represents a female version of the almighty god of Judaism, Christianity, or Islam. They can't get past patriarchal notions of male supremacy and imagine a world where a female spirit was venerated in just the same way. Yet that is what the evidence shows: spiritual activity taking place in the belly of the earth; with symbols of the vulva central to activities there; with statues of the faceless goddess carried from camp to camp; or carried as a pendant around the neck. These people turned to a female creatrix for reassurance, hope, and support in times more dangerous and precarious than we could imagine. If we find it unbelievable that people would ever turn to a female deity, does that show our inability to recognise what is in front of us because of our patriarchal prejudice? Are we so deeply imbued in patriarchal mind-sets that we simply cannot imagine another way of experiencing the world? If so, we need to extricate ourselves from the cultural experience in which we are mired or we will never understand the potential variety of human thought. In particular, we may never free our minds to find new forms of male-female relationships.

SELECTED REFERENCES:
https://www.nature.com/nature/videoarchive/prehistoricpinup, accessed April 2017.
Malinowski, Bronislaw, *The Sexual Life of Savages in North Western Melanesia*, 3rd Edn., London: George Routledge and Sons, 1939, pages 155 and 156.

39: THE POWER OF BLOOD: LIFE AND DEATH

If men bleed it means they have been wounded, and might die. But all women bleed, and it indicates life. Not only do they bleed harmlessly each month, when women give birth it's accompanied by blood, and the deep red placenta. Red thus became the colour of women, symbolic of their ability to bring forth life.

Some Native American cultures considered menstrual blood to be sacred, as Paula Gunn Allen explains:

"The water of life, menstrual or postpartum blood, was held sacred. Sacred often means taboo; that is, what is empowered in a ritual sense is not to be touched or approached by any who are weaker than the power itself, lest they suffer negative consequences from contact. The blood of woman was in and of itself infused with the power of Supreme Mind, and so women were held in awe and respect."

Aboriginal Australian myth says that red ochre was created where the female ancestors dropped their menstrual blood. The people wandering the icy wastes of Europe and Eurasia may have thought it had another origin, but they used red ochre in abundance. It was used to decorate the walls of caves deep inside the ground, and it was placed on and around bodies of people laid in graves.

Not only did red ochre represent life, it also encompassed the idea that death can lead to rebirth and regeneration. We can guess this from the innumerable ritual contexts in which red ochre was used. Above all, it covered people in their graves. In Austria, around 25,000 BC, two babies were sprinkled with ochre before being wrapped in a skin and placed in their grave. Someone put a necklace made of mammoth ivory in with them, and carefully covered the grave with a mammoth shoulder blade. The care taken with this burial is not unusual; we find the same thing at many other sites from this early time.

We know that red ochre was important to people from at least 100,000 years ago because a workshop for producing it was found at the Blombos Cave on the southern shore of South Africa. Archaeologist Dr Christopher Henshilwood and his team found two abalone shells full of red ochre, as well as grindstones and hammer-stones that were part of the toolkit used to process it. From this same site we have the oldest decorated objects yet found, thought to be at least 75,000 years old – two pieces of red ochre with flat surfaces incised with a complex geometric pattern. At least 8,000 other pieces of ochre have been found at this site.

From earliest times red ochre was the primary ritualistic requirement all over the world, which is why ancient peoples often made their homes near deposits of it. The tradition carried on for tens of thousands of years. Even as late as 4,500 BC in Sardinia, people were buried in the foetal position and covered in red ochre. In one grave, next to a female figurine, archaeologists found two halves of an open shell filled with red ochre. In the hypogeum at Hal Saflieni in Malta – an underground complex of many rooms dated between 4,000-2,500 BC – the excarnated bones (with flesh removed) of between six and seven thousand people were found, all amply covered in red ochre.

It is of course difficult to know why, for such a huge span of time, it was important for people to be covered in red ochre on their death. The most obvious explanation would be that, by replicating the redness of the blood that accompanies birth, a person would be reborn in the afterlife. Red ochre may also have been about power, and decoration, but from earliest times it was at the centre of ritual and spiritual life, and associated with womanhood.

SELECTED REFERENCES:
Allen, Paula Gunn, *The Sacred Hoop*, 1986, page 28. Copyright © 1986, 1992 by Paula Gunn Allen. Reprinted by permission of Beacon Press, Boston.

40: HUNTING MAGIC

The idea that prehistoric women were confined to the 'sex = fertility = mother' box conflicts with the archaeological record. Artwork and graves show us that women were also highly respected because of their role in magic, particularly hunting magic. Women are shown in hunting scenes on engraved bone objects found at La Vache and La Madeleine, and on hunting tools at Rond-du-Barry and Saut du Perron.

The oldest confirmed grave of a shaman was found at Hilazon Tachit, in present day Israel, and is dated to around 10,000 BC. There, a Natufian woman of about 45 years of age was buried with extraordinary care in a specially made walled grave. She was buried with 50 complete tortoise shells, a large human foot, a bowl, and parts of various animals – one part of each animal: the pelvis of a leopard; the forearm of a wild boar; the horn core of a gazelle; the tail vertebrae of an auroch (an extinct cattle); the bony wing part of a golden eagle; and the skulls of two stone martens (a kind of weasel). The archaeologists who discovered the grave say "the evidence suggests that this woman held a unique position in the community."

Another female shaman was found at Bad Durrenberg in central Germany, and is dated to around 7,000 BC. Even now, the bed of red ochre she was found on is 7 inches (30cm) deep. A reconstruction of the arrangement of bones around her head and body shows that she was wearing an animal head-dress. Again, a variety of animal bones were found, along with teeth and shells. These include parts of a crane, beaver, red deer, roe deer, swamp turtles, and freshwater mussels. Also buried with her were an infant less than a year old, decorative plaques made of boar tusk, 2 bone needles, a hoe made of the antler of a deer, and 31 tiny flint blades held in a container made of the hollow bone of a crane. The connection between this woman and hunting magic could not be clearer.

A later example of a female shaman burial comes from Samborzec in Poland, dated around 5,000 BC. Here the woman's skull has remnants of red ochre, and she was wearing a belt of animal teeth and bones.

These graves broadly fall into the Mesolithic – an archaeological period between the old hunter-gather societies of the Upper Paleolithic, the ice age, and the more recent farming communities of the Neolithic. The dates for the Mesolithic vary widely, depending on the area and stage of development. The question is, were there female shamans before the Mesolithic, and after?

One grave dated around 25,000 BC that probably belonged to a female shaman was found in Dolni Vestonice, in the Czech Republic. At that time it was a settlement of about 100 people – mammoth hunters living close to the ice cap. Under the floor of a large hut archaeologists found the body, protected by two mammoth shoulder bones. She had been sprinkled in red ochre, and buried holding an arctic fox in one hand and ten canine fox teeth in the other. A flint spearhead was also found.

There is speculation that this woman was involved in the manufacture of tiny clay figurines, mostly animals, baked in a kiln in a nearby hut. 2,300 fragments have been found. One lion head figurine had a deliberately-made hole in it, giving the impression the animal figurines were made, then 'killed' or destroyed, as a form of sympathetic magic to bring success in the hunt.

Another piece of evidence for female shamans, dated around 8,000 BC, comes from La Madeleine rock shelter in France. On a small limestone pebble two figures have been engraved, both wearing animal masks. They are seen from the side angle and one has a breast, so can be identified as female. The gender of the other is unknown, as there is no breast or penis shown, but is assumed to be male.

Shamans have high status because they seem able to communicate with the spirit world. Primitive societies always respect the environment in which they live, seeing spirits in trees for example, and animals as having spirits. The shamans from this time needed somehow to identify with the animals, either to get into the mind of the animal to make the kill easier, or even apologise in advance for the kill which is about to take place. Of course we have no idea of what was actually in the mind of people at this time, but we can guess that shamans were also healers, fortune-tellers, and magicians. They had knowledge of the spirit world unavailable to others in the group, and this gave them special status.

Another aspect of hunting magic appears to centre on menstrual blood, specifically that it exerted a power that could affect the outcome of the hunt. At Tiout, in the Saharan Atlas Mountains in Algeria, a rock engraving shows a woman with upraised arms, a line extending from her vagina to the penis of a hunter who has his bow and arrow poised ready to shoot at an ostrich **(Fig. 6)**. This could be interpreted as woman's transformative powers symbolised by menstrual blood, being passed to the hunting man, so that he too may have power over life and death and, during the hunt, bring the animal down, bleeding. This image has been dated to around 2,000 BC, when people had started farming. That shows that the female was still being respected as a transformative force well into the Neolithic Age.

Fig. 6. Algerian stone drawing, Tiout, Atlas Mountains, North Africa.

Although archaeologists invariably assume that any non-gendered image that looks like a shaman must be male, historical and contemporary anthropological records do not support that view. At Astuvansalmi in Finland there's a 3,000 BC cave painting of a woman hunting elk with a bow and arrow. She may have been a woman out hunting, a shaman, or an early version of Tellervo, the Finnish goddess of the forest. During the Chinese Shang dynasty in the 2nd millennium BC, women took shamanic roles. Women have traditionally been shamans in the Nanai culture that today has 12,000 members in Russia and 4,600 across the border in north eastern China. In the ethnic Korean religion of Muism, which has around 10 million followers today, the shamans are both male and female. Among the San of South Africa until quite recently, a third of the women were shamans, as were half the men. Shamanism is not, and probably never was, an exclusively male pursuit.

SELECTED REFERENCES:
Grosman, Leore, Munro, Natalie D., Belfer-Cohen, Anna, 'A 12,000-year-old Shaman burial from the southern Levant (Israel)', Proceedings of the National Academy of Sciences, November 18 2008, Volume 105, No. 46, 17665-17669.

Porr, M. and Alt, K.W. (2006), The burial of Bad Durrenberg, Central Germany: osteopathology and osteoarchaeology of a late Mesolithic shaman's grave. International Journal of Osteoarchaeology, 16: 395-406. Doi:10.1002/oa.839

Hansen, Svend, 'Grave of a female in Bad Durrenberg' in exhibition catalogue 'Archaeological Finds From Germany', Berlin 2010, pages 20-21.

Clottes, Jean, and Lewis-Williams, David, 'The Shamans of Prehistory', New York: Harry N. Abrams Inc., 1998, page 23.

41: THE FIRST REVOLUTION

The first revolution in reproduction theory happened when people started thinking about the power of seeds. And the first thing anyone learns about seeds is that they need water. This is when men began to be seen as important in reproduction because they had the 'water' in their penises that women needed to make the seeds within them germinate and grow. The agricultural revolution ushered in the female-seed theory of reproduction.

When previously nomadic people stop following herds of animals around and settle down in one place, they're in a position to observe the way seeds work: a wild bean or seed dropped on the ground can, after some time, and plenty of rain, sprout into life and produce more beans or seeds. This is what was happening in 10,000 BC, as people laid claim to their traditional area of resource exploitation, aware perhaps that other people had their eyes on it. Population pressures, possibly caused by climate changes at the time, may have led to the agricultural revolution.

When people settled in Hallan Cemi in eastern Turkey in 10,000 BC, they were there all year round eating clams and sea clubrush from the nearby river, a range of meats including wild sheep, goats, deer and boar, wild lettuce, mullein, beans, peas, vetch and other legumes, almond and pistachio nuts, dock from the buckwheat family, barley, and small-seeded grasses, all nicely flavoured with the medicinal herb *Ziziphora tenuior*. They had pestles and mortars, querns and hand stones, so we know they were grinding plants to make flour or oil. There's no evidence they farmed as such, but the people of Hallan Cemi probably noticed that beans and seeds are not just consumable food; they have the potential to grow into plants laden with more beans and seeds – foods for the future.

Social links between Hallan Cemi and the village of Mureybet, two hundred miles west, are indicated by similarities in their architecture and decoration of objects. Now hidden under the waters of Lake Assad in northern Syria due to the building of a dam, Mureybet had four layers of habitation from which archaeologists can see the transition from simply gathering wild seed, to actually planting it – particularly einkorn, rye, and barley. This was the beginning of agriculture. And when they weren't working in the field, the people in Mureybet were making figurines of women in limestone and baked earth.

Significantly, the figurines were found in Building 47, which was at the centre of communal life in Mureybet. Unlike the residential houses, Building 47 had been sunken into the ground and built with 'cells' that delineated activities carried out there: food storage; storage of new bone and flint tools; the tool shop; mortars and querns for grinding; cooking facilities; and an area with a bench for meetings. Only 8 figurines were found in the village – the gender of one couldn't be identified, but the other 7 were female. And the fact that they were housed in Building 47, at the centre of social and working life, gives the impression that the female was closely associated with seed and fertility.

Just 30 miles (or 50 km) from Mureybet, on the Euphrates

River, was Abu Hureyra, now also under Lake Assad. It was first occupied in 11,000 BC and is credited with being the place where farming began, with the cultivation of rye. Farming probably began in several places at the same time but, in any event, it's clear that by around 10,000 BC people knew that the grain they could eat was, at the same time, seed they could grow.

As far as wheat is concerned, the epicentre of the agricultural revolution in the 'Fertile Crescent' is thought to be around the Karaca Dag mountain near the town of Sanliurfa (Urfa) in south-east Turkey, because the genetically-common ancestor of 68 strains of wheat grown today can be traced back to there. This whole region is thought to be the source not only of einkorn, but also of emmer wheat. Both species have been found in the nearby site of Cafer Hoyuk, settled in 8,920 BC, and in Cayonu dated 7,200 BC. Einkorn has also been found at Nevali Cori, occupied in 9,000 BC.

There were stylistic, ritualistic, or architectural links between all these sites in northern Syria and south-eastern Turkey, as well as trade in raw materials such as phosphates and obsidian and finished objects such flint blades and chlorite bowls. Other interesting places in this local network were Mezraa-Teleilat, where a number of male figurines have been found, and Jerf el Ahmar. Communities were thriving in this area, between the northern tributaries of the Euphrates and Tigris rivers, and knowledge about the power of seeds was likely being shared.

The present day town of Sanliurfa (Urfa) is right in the middle of all this activity and settlement, and this is where archaeologists excavated a life-size limestone sculpture called 'Balikli Gol man' (or 'Urfa Man'), dated to around 10,000 BC. He stands with his arms by his side, with both hands pointing inwards, as if drawing attention to his penis. This sculpture announces the significance of men to reproduction. If he was the first rain god, he would be the first of many.

Just 10 miles (16 km) away is a spectacular archaeological find that has completely rewritten history. Dated at 9,500-8,000 BC and probably earlier at the unexcavated levels, Göbekli Tepe is 7,000 years *older* than Stonehenge and the Egyptian pyramids at Giza. Excavation began in 1994 and today only 10% of the site has yet been uncovered, so it's impossible to say what will eventually be found. What we do know from excavations and ground penetrating radar is that there are 20 stone wall circles and rectangles, and over 200 stones standing up to 20 feet (6m) high. The circles are between 10-30 meters in diameter, and built into the walls are T-shaped standing stones, with two further standing stones in the middle. Each pillar is carved in low relief, and skillfully decorated with a variety of dangerous animals and insects, particularly snakes. On two pillars, arms and hands have been sculpted in low relief, resting above a belt and loincloth. The stones have no facial features, and nothing to indicate their gender. Given the high quality of carving at the site, these omissions are deliberate and suggest these pillars represent beings that have human characteristics, but are above them or distinct from them in some way – ancestors or spiritual beings. There are no domestic artefacts at the site, only feasting debris, making this the earliest known major centre of communal spiritual activity.

Several small sculptures from Göbekli and nearby sites are of men with large penises, and it is clear that the phallus has taken on a significance it did not have in earlier times. One small ithyphallic man is carved on a pillar, with his head missing. This imagery is to do with an association between human skulls and vultures that will be seen again thousands of years later, and pertains to ideas about death, rather than life. Nevertheless, male imagery suddenly makes an appearance from 10,000 BC in several places, alongside continuing imagery of the female.

In a rectangular enclosure at Göbekli, archaeologists found a 30 cm (1 foot) long image of a woman engraved on a horizontal slab of stone placed between two pillars decorated with lions. The fact that she is placed between two felines is interesting, given that images of a woman between two felines is a theme that can be seen throughout the Neolithic over a huge geographical area. Her entire body is shown, and she is described as squatting but looks as if she is lying on her back with her legs splayed out. Something is either going into, or out of, her vagina. It looks like several penis shapes, or a great deal of liquid. If it shows childbirth, the baby's legs rather than its head are coming out of her body. Archaeologists have variously described her as 'ready for coitus', 'menstruating', or say this slab of stone is where ritual sex took place. This activity was so well known throughout ancient time there's a name for it – *heiros gamos*. It's when people have sex in public – and that could be one man with one woman, or one woman with several men. Maybe people at Göbeki were watching women invite men to water the seed inside them, so it could germinate and grow.

SELECTED REFERENCES:
Ibanez, Juan Jose, (Ed.), Le Site Neolithique de Tell Mureybet (Northern Syria), British Archaeological Reports, 2008, p661-677.
Schmidt, Klaus, *Sie bauten die ersten Tempel,* Munich: Deutscher Taschenbuch Verlag, 2008.

42: WOMAN'S PERENNIAL SEED

Eight and a half thousand years ago in Çatalhöyük, Turkey, someone pushed a seed into a small clay female figurine before firing it in an oven. The idea conveyed by this action is that the seed is within women. In fact, this is true – every baby girl is born with the seeds of her children, the ova, within her. If people at that time ago thought men 'watered' female seed, their theory differs from our own reproduction theory only in that we know the male role to be genomic imprinting of the seed rather than 'watering'.

When the potential of plant seed was discovered there was a momentous change in human lifestyle and development. People realised the seed was everything: with it, life continues; without it, they starved. At some point early in the agricultural revolution, people wondered if humans also began as seeds. They were coming from the ancient understanding that women reproduced on their own, so would have expected the seed to be in them. After all, babies are pulled from women as fruits are pulled from trees, or roots are pulled from the earth. Certainly, people in the Neolithic wouldn't be thinking in terms of two seeds and fusion (like ovum and sperm) because seeds are singular: one seed grows into one plant, laden with more seed. Nowhere would they see plants growing from two seeds that had been squished together. It would be entirely logical for them to think the seed lay dormant in the woman until it was 'watered' by the semen of the male, just as perennial seeds lie dormant in the earth until rain stimulates them into germinating and growing.

Archaeologists don't talk about reproduction theory. I can say that because I've spoken to dozens of them, and read hundreds of their books. When I ask them about the people they study – "where did they think babies come from?" – the archaeologists have no idea what I'm even talking about. Apparently, like so many other people, they think people have always known the facts of life. It is curious to me that while anthropologists routinely talk about 'kinship systems', which explores where people come from, archaeologists seem to think everyone has always known the facts of life, which they assume to be the same as ours – there are two parents who make an equal contribution to the child. But if they knew anything about the history of embryology, they'd know that before 1900 AD nobody had the faintest idea where babies come from, and that what we have from history and prehistory is one big mistake after the other. Archaeologists seriously need to think about reproduction theory because, as Ashley Montagu wrote in *Coming Into Being Among The Australian Aborigines*:

"procreative beliefs are the starting point of family systems, social organisation, religion, and world view."

Reproduction theory, or procreative beliefs, are pivotal, and if archaeologists thought about it for two minutes they'd be in an infinitely better position to understand the cultures they study.

When faced with thousands of images of Neolithic female figures from all over the world, archaeologists usually refer to them as images associated with "fertility" or "fecundity" – the potential for fertility. But both these phrases are meaningless in terms of reproduction theory. It makes a great deal of difference if you think, as we do, that both male and female contribute 'seed,' or if you think the seed comes from the male testicles and is planted in the seedless female soil, or if you think the female is the source of seed and the man waters it, or if you think the woman is parthenogenetic and reproduces without men. The term "fertility" can be applied to women in all these cases, but each variation has profound impact on the relative value given to women, and to men, and the way society organises around those fundamental ideas.

The so-called "fertility figurines" were not just about bringing good luck to the crop in the fields, or about women having babies. They reflected the fact that people conceptualised women as the source of human seed. And that idea leads directly to the veneration of female ancestors, from whom they came, and to the notion of an original female creatrix, the source of all life on earth. As the originator and giver of life, the creatrix would also have power over death. Using the phrase "fertility figurines" locks the female into the sex/baby/mother box rather than into the life and death/creativity/power box. But there is an existential difference between these two concepts, and making a distinction between them is important.

Whereas in the pre-farming Palaeolithic era the female images are in a class of their own without male counterparts, and without facial features, Neolithic societies valued both male and female for their role in reproduction, and their representations show faces characteristic of the location and historical period from which they were uncovered. In the earliest writings it is clear there was a marriage between the sky god – the god of thunder and rain – and the earth goddess. But as the source of the seed, the female was in the more creative position.

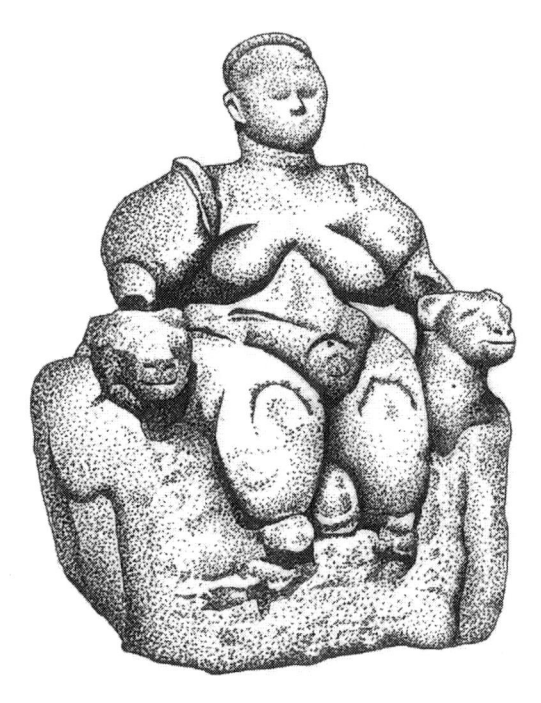

Fig. 7. Çatalhöyük Goddess, Turkey, baked clay, 18cm high.

Çatalhöyük is a large archaeological site in Turkey that has been in the process of excavation on and off for 70 years. Covering over 33 acres, it housed up to 8,000 people between 7,400 – 6,000 BC, and has provided us with an exceptional amount of data. As well as the female figurine with a seed inside her, one of the most interesting finds is an impressive, large-breasted female figurine sitting with both her hands resting on the heads of two large cats – thought to be leopards **(Fig. 7)**. Like many other female figurines, she had been placed in a "grain" (or seed) storage bin. The tails of the leopards curl over her back and rest on her shoulders, giving the overall impression that she is in control of them, and they are comfortable with her.

In 2016 two stone female figurines were found close to each other in an unusually large building. Both are complete and undamaged. The larger, at 7 inches (17cm) high, portrays an older woman; the other, at 2.7 inches (7cm) high, portrays a young woman and has two holes in the head, from which the figurine could be suspended, perhaps to be used as a pendant.

A particularly remarkable find from this site is a figurine depicting a woman with her hands resting on breasts above a distended abdomen with a protruding navel as if pregnant, while her back is sculpted in skeletal form complete with vertebrae, ribs, and scapulae. This conjunction of life and death imagery says something profound about womanhood, whether that is an intimate connection to ancestors, a role in rebirth after death, or some other concept we cannot imagine.

Leopards play a very significant role in the story of Çatalhöyük because although they feature in about 65% of the paintings, and 35% of the reliefs, no bones have been found. This indicates there was a taboo regarding them: although leopard skins seem to have been used in clothing, removing the skins from the bodies of leopards must have been done off-site. (By comparison, 56% of the bones found on site are from sheep, but there are no paintings of them). However, there is one small piece of leopard and it was found in a unique context: a claw had been drilled to make a hole so it could be used as pendant; this pendant was found in the grave of an older woman; who clasped to her chest a skull that had been plastered and painted red 3 times. This unusual skull was originally thought to be male, but is now classed as likely female. Was this the grave of a woman of particular value, indicated by her leopard claw pendant, holding her female ancestor?

The imagery from Çatalhöyük tells a story of women being the source of human seed, the protectors of plant seed in storage, people with special power and value, with an association with both life and death. Çatalhöyük was an extremely complex society that worked hard to emphasise equality between people, yet in the most significant finds it's the female that features. But, because the female had respect in Çatalhöyük that doesn't mean the male did not. The difference between a female-seed life view and a male-seed life view (the legacy of which we're still dealing with today) is that in the former the woman is both the source of the seed and the means of producing it, so she does not need to control the man, whereas in the male-seed theory the source of the seed is in the male but the means of production is the female, leading men to think they needed to assure their means of reproduction by controlling women. In Çatalhöyük there was no need for one human being to control another for reproductive purposes, and the people there existed peacefully for 1,400 years.

There are hundreds of Neolithic sites and each tells its own story and has unique cultural methods of expressing the idea that the female is the source of seed. The 2½ inch (6cm) Trento figurine from Italy, made from bone and decorated with ochre, had been incised to indicate a seed in place of the vagina and the plant branches over the abdomen **(Fig. 8)**. Around the same time in western Ukraine, people were making female figurines which they decorated by pressing grain seeds into the terracotta. In Harappa, a city built by the Sarasvati-Indus Civilisation in present day Pakistan, a seal dated 3,000 BC shows a woman with a plant coming out of her vagina. The visual association between women and seed took many forms but told the same story – women have the seed within them.

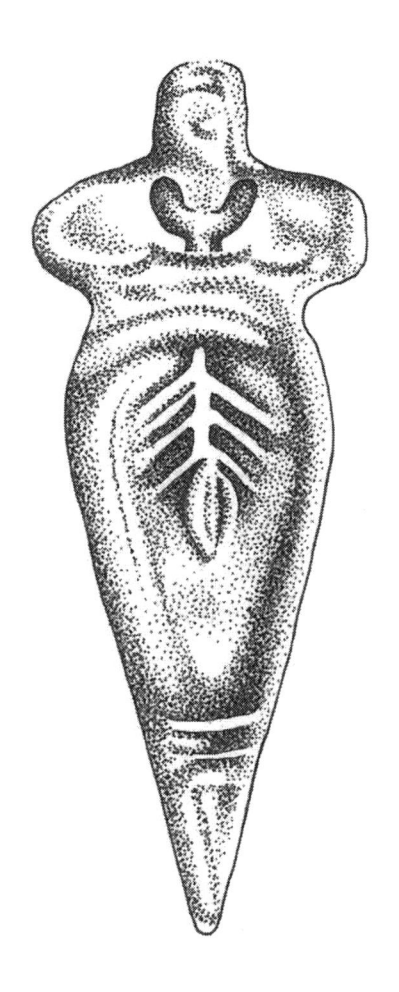

Fig. 8. Trento figurine, 4,500 BC, engraving on bone, painted with ochre, 6cm high, Gaban cave, near Trento, northern Italy.

SELECTED REFERENCES

Montagu, Ashley, *Coming Into Being Among the Australian Aborigines*, New York: E.P. Dutton & Company, 1938.

Hodder, Ian, *Çatalhöyük, The Leopard's Tale*, London: Thames and Hudson, 2011.

Boz, B, Hager, L.D. 'Living Above the Dead: Intramural Burial Practices at Çatalhöyük' in *Humans and Landscapes of Çatalhöyük: Reports from the 2000-2008 Seasons*, I. Hodder (ed.), Vol. 8, Monograph 47, London: British Institute at Ankara, 2013.

43: MAN THE WATERER

When people realised the importance of seed, they also realised the importance of water to the seed. Without water, seeds don't germinate and grow. With water, seeds start to sprout little shoots and grow and grow until they are themselves producing lots of seed. Men must have been ecstatic when they realised they had something to do with reproduction. Before the agricultural revolution they thought women reproduced on their own. It turned out that women needed them. Finally, men could say they had a role in that greatest mystery – life. But, although men were important to reproduction, they were secondary. They were helpmates to women who, as the source of seed, where still the parents – from whence life came.

If people thought men watered the seed in the woman we'd expect them to have water gods, particularly thunder gods who explode and release their shower, like ejaculation. We'd also expect to find earth goddesses who become fertile after that shower of rain. And that's exactly what we do have. This duality is one of the classic creation themes of all time, and the earliest. It doesn't tell us what happened in the wordless early Neolithic, but it gives us a clue as to how things may have been.

There have been thousands of thunder and rain gods, from China to Scandinavia, from Nigeria to Brazil, from every corner of Europe and the Middle East, to Japan, India, Polynesia, Native America, Mexico, Finland, and just about anywhere you care to mention. The names we know them by today include Ba'al/Hadad/Iškur, Indra, Zeus, Perun, Thor, Take-Mikazuchi, Denka, Tlaloc, Wollungua, Lono, and many others. There have been so many 'earth goddesses', it would take a book to list them. Tara, known under different names from Ireland to Tibet (Taranis, Turan, Terah, Terra Mater etc.), was one ancient goddess who was fertilised by rain from the gods. In Wales and Ireland Tara was fertilised by Taran and Torann, respectively, their names both meaning 'thunder.' Early representations of water gods show them holding thunderbolts in their hands, with water gushing from their shoulders, offering libations to the earth goddess, or being surrounded by water in their watery realm.

The earliest culture to provide us with the written word is Sumer – the land between and around the southern end of the Tigris and Euphrates rivers, in present day Iraq. Although it's often spoken about as one static culture, Sumer changed profoundly over its 3,000 year history, between 5,000 BC and 1,800 BC. (It then lasted almost 1,000 years longer within the larger area known as Mesopotamia). In Sumerian, the words 'a' and 'Ab' mean both 'water' and 'semen'. This may indicate that the meaning of 'water' changed over a period of time, coming also to mean 'semen'.

This makes deciphering ancient Sumerian texts difficult because many translators project onto the words 'a' and 'Ab' what they expect it to mean. So, for example, when the god Enki fills the rivers Tigris and Euphrates with something gushing from his penis they translate 'a' as 'water', but when he's having sex with a goddess 'a' becomes 'semen'. Maybe the Sumerians meant Enki was 'watering' the goddess, but as the Sumerian words for 'water' and 'semen' are the same, we just don't know.

In Sumerian mythology there was an original creation goddess called Nammu. She gave birth to Ki, the earth goddess, and An, the sky god. The land receives little rainfall so, to take advantage of the rich alluvial soil left by the annual flood, the Sumerians invented irrigation. It's thought they did this in Eridu which, dating from 5,000 BC, was perhaps the oldest city of all. Despite later rivalry between the fourteen major towns of Sumer, Eridu was always mentioned in lists first, as if it had some special and ancient religious significance.

Eridu grew around a cultic site where, beneath the altar, archaeologists found a bowl filled with appliqué snakes, and clay coils, possibly representing snakes. Snakes feature in many religious cults because by shedding their dead skins in one piece they appear, symbolically, reborn. There's no evidence of either male gods or female goddesses from the earliest layers of the site, although a 4,500 BC baked clay female figurine was found here, and at many other locations around – the so-called Ubaid figurines. Most figurines are female although male examples do exist. Later on in Eridu's history it became associated with the god Enki, who is interesting because he had intercourse with many goddesses. The question is, what did that intercourse represent – the delivery of water to the female seed, or the delivery of seed itself?

A study of Enki from the earliest Sumerian times to the later epic myths 3,000 years later has been carried out by Peeter Espak of the University of Tartu in Estonia. He shows that while in the later period Enki is credited with creating the minor gods and goddesses, and being involved in the creation of humans, Enki does neither of these things in earlier texts. Espak also points out that, near the end of the Ur III dynasty, Enki's position in the pantheon of gods and goddesses has been elevated from fourth to third, putting him above the mother-goddess. Espak writes:

"The possibility of female dominance in early and more archaic stages of religion is certainly imaginable. It is possible to assume that also the ancient divine power in Eridu must have been female in gender, and by later developments caused by the growth of male dominance in society general, the original female deity was replaced by a male one. However, the statement about Enki being a universal male reproductive element in the early pantheon can not be confirmed to be based on any known source."

Enki's role changed over time after "the growth of male dominance," when the liquid coming from his penis became associated with semen. But from earliest times Enki was associated with water and his watery underground domain, known as Abzu. Cylinder seals show him with two rivers flowing from his shoulders, as he sits surrounded by rivers on each side. In Sumer, the water from the rivers flooded annually and gave fertility to the soil and, as Espak notes, the "connection between Enki's sexuality and the irrigation of the land seems to be very strong."

Another Sumerian god was Damuzi (later, Tammuz), the most famous consort of the goddess Inanna (later, Ishtar). Damuzi was known as 'the Quickener of the Child'. Aside from meaning 'to hasten or accelerate', the verb 'to quicken' means 'to give, add or restore to a person or thing' – and we can see Damuzi as adding that which restores life to the seed within the woman. The word also means 'to animate, stimulate, excite or inspire', and while Damuzi was certainly venerated for doing these things, he was not venerated above the female. The scholar Edwin O. James described him as a "subordinate satellite" of "the Mother Goddess," saying: "... in the last analysis Innana-Ishtar, not Dumuzi-Tammuz was the ultimate and constant source of regeneration, Dumuzi-Tammuz being only instrumental in the process as her agent." This was not a relationship of equals: "when he was brought into close connection with Ishtar in the Tammuz myth, he was her son as well as her lover and brother, and always subordinate to her as the Young god."

Early Sumerian male gods were not superior to the females. On the contrary, the females were dominant in the relationship. Only one thing can account for that – she was the generant. A man might provide the water, but the seed came from her. That made her the source of life, not him.

Looking at the wordless past we see many examples of men and gods associated with water, nets and fish. The Sumerian water god Enki was sometimes depicted garmented in fish skin, while on the Mediterranean island of Crete 'The Harvester's Vase' was found showing a man in a fish-scale cape leading the procession back from harvesting the fields. He may have been a priest as images of fish-clothed priests can be seen on artefacts elsewhere for at least another thousand years. Also from Crete is the mysterious 'Phaistos Disk' which has pictographs arranged in spirals on both sides. At the centre of one side there's the classic ancient sign for 'water' – the wavy line, and what looks like a fig – a fruit bursting with seed. Does this say that life begins with the combination of seed and water?

Fig. 9. Late Minoan goddess or priestess, clay figurine, 31 inches (79cm) high, Gazi, Crete.

Crete was the centre of the Minoan civilisation that ran from 3,650 to 1,400 BC, and may have been the last of the female-centred societies. They had no male gods, only female goddesses – including the snake goddess, the lady of the beasts, and the mountain mother. Some experts believe all were manifestations of one all-powerful earth mother. Women dominated the priesthood; they were administrators; and participated equally with men in the local sport – facing a charging bull, grabbing the horns, and leaping over the bull's back. The Minoans had a vast trading industry, but no weapons. The civilisation came to an abrupt end when their trading centre on the island of Thera (now called Santorini), was blown sky high by a massive volcanic eruption that also created a tsunami which destroyed the fleet and engulfed Crete itself. Volcanic ash then descended on the island and proceeded to kill off the vegetation and animals. The refugees made their way to the west coast of Turkey where they settled, still following their matrilineal traditions. Matrilineal societies trace their ancestry along the female line, following the female seed.

  The catastrophic events at Crete brought to an abrupt end the last great culture to venerate the female, and would have profoundly shaken and undermined the notion of a protective female deity. Elsewhere, the male-seed theology had essentially taken over. But this is not to say vestiges of the female-centred religions did not still continue. At the time, nobody could prove where human seed came from one way or the other – maybe it was from the male, maybe it was from the female. There was only logic, not proof, and the logic could be bent either way. This led to ideological conflict that continued for many centuries and, also, to the 'hedging of bets' – people worshipping both male and female deities.

  The history of reproduction theory makes it very plain that people in different places, and at different times, can come to a wide variety of 'truths' when faced with the same facts. For example, when the existence of a female seed was denied, it was said that ovaries provide lubrication for the act of intercourse, or food for the baby growing within the woman. It is possible that during the female-seed era some people thought the liquid coming from the penis wasn't 'water' but a kind of compost – a substance that is not seed but does contribute to growth.

SELECTED REFERENCES:
Espak, Peeter, Ancient Near Eastern Gods Enki and Ea: Diachronical Analysis of Texts and Images from the Earliest Sources to the Neo-Sumerian Period, Master's Thesis, Tartu University, Faculty of Theology, Chair for Ancient Near Eastern Studies, 2006, pages 13 and 122.
James, Edwin Oliver, *The Ancient Gods: The History and Diffusion of Religion in the Ancient Near East and the Eastern Mediterranean*, London: Weidenfeld and Nicolson, 1960, quotes from pages, in order, 304 and 80.

44: THE EGG

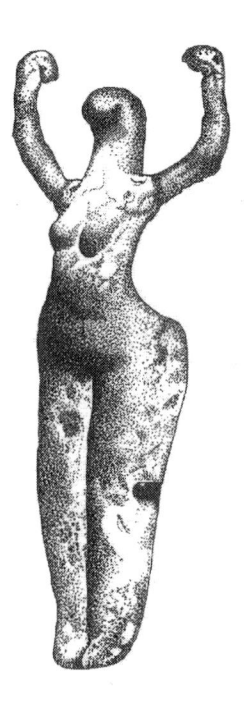

Fig. 10. Predynastic Egyptian terracotta figurine
with bird head and upraised arms.

During the Neolithic female figurines were sometimes associated with birds and eggs. They had the bodies of women and the heads of birds, or eggs painted on them. Only females lay eggs. Although females of the human species don't lay eggs they, and other mammals, carry the foetus within a membranous sack not unlike the membrane on the inner side of an eggshell. People at this time didn't know that birds can migrate half way around the world to feed and stay for months, then come back. They just saw that the birds were there one day, and gone the next. But they did return, as if they'd come back to life again. The bird, the egg, and all they represented in terms of re-birth was linked to the female form.

Eggs appear on Neolithic vessels of all sorts, and people also produced small egg-shaped burial jars. In Malta, Sicily, Sardinia and other Mediterranean areas, egg-shaped tombs were hewn out of solid rock. The use of the egg shape in death-related activity indicates that the egg was associated not only with birth, but with regeneration – being re-created in the afterlife.

45: ANIMAL HUSBANDRY

It is often assumed that once people started domesticating animals they would understand animal reproduction, and from there get a better understanding of human reproduction. We know in the later, male-seed, era people realised that with no ram, there would be no lamb. But that thought is by no means inevitable or universal. Animal husbandry, in itself, tells us no more about human reproduction than human intercourse does. People just tend to project onto their animals life-views gained elsewhere. In the female-seed era they would have thought the ram watered the ewe, and that's why there were lambs.

The Trobriand Islanders, who think men's only role in reproduction is to keep the vagina open and lubricated so the baby can come out, were asked by the anthropologist Malinowski about their pigs. They kept three kinds of pig: the domesticated – which is a delicacy; bush-pig – the eating of which was taboo; and the imported – which cost between five and ten domesticated pigs. So inter-breeding was certainly a matter of concern. The Trobrianders, however, come from the position that "The female pig breeds by itself" meaning without a hog, or even pig-spirit. Consequently, inter-breeding was of no concern and the Trobrianders allowed their domesticated pigs to wander into the bush, where they mated with wild pigs. When Malinowski suggested they were eating the results of inter-breeding (taboo pig), the Trobrianders simply didn't know what he was talking about. One native told him: "From all male pigs we cut off the testes" (to fatten them) "They copulate not. Yet the females bring forth." As Malinowski notes:

"Thus he ignored the possible misconduct of the bush-pigs and adduced the castration of domestic hogs as final proof that intercourse has nothing to do with breeding."

This proves the point that 'logic' can be bent to prove any point of view. Animal husbandry does not inevitably provide a lesson in the facts of life, any more than human intercourse does.

In the biblical story, Jacob wanted payment from Laban for working for him for fourteen years and Laban agreed that Jacob could take the animals that were striped, speckled and spotted white. So Jacob set about manipulating the stock. He stripped part of the bark of hazel, green poplar and chestnut branches, revealing some of the white beneath, and placed them in the watering troughs. His purpose in doing this was so:

"they should conceive when they came to drink; And the flocks conceived before the rods, and brought forth cattle ringstraked, speckled, and spotted." (Genesis 30: 35-42)

Jacob is talking here about males mounting females as they drank and, coming from the male-seed tradition, would be thinking the males deliver seed into the females. Presumably he also thought that if, while this was happening, the cows saw spotted or striped white images they would somehow transfer those patterns to the offspring, making them striped or speckled and spotted white. This passage proves that even 7,000 years after animal husbandry had begun, people had bizarre notions about how inheritance worked.

SELECTED REFERENCES:
Malinowski, Bronislaw, *The Sexual Life of Savages in North-Western Melanesia*, 3rd Edition, London: George Routledge & Sons, 1939, page 162.

46: THEY MADE LOVE, NOT WAR

There is a lot of archaeological evidence from the Neolithic and it shows that people during the female-seed era were egalitarian and peaceful. They were buried without any evidence of violent death. The settlements had no defensive walls and the housing was more or less equal in terms of size and belongings. Archaeologists don't find weapons of war. And when settlements were abandoned it wasn't because they had been destroyed or the people violently killed. All this is in sharp contrast to what would happen later when the male-seed patriarchal era introduced social division, violence and terror.

Control is the issue that differentiates female-seed and male-seed societies. When women are believed to be the only source of seed and human life, and watered by men, women do not need to control men to reproduce themselves. They just need to have sex with them. On the other hand, when men thought they were the deliverers of human seed into the 'soil' of women, they felt the need to control the means of their own reproduction: women. One life-view does not involve the concept of control, while the other does. These are profoundly different way of relating, human being to human being, and it surely led to new, more controlling, ways of thinking.

The male-seed theory also leads to the idea that a man needs to 'sow his oats' to increase the number of his children – which improves his potential for wealth, and security in old age. As men do not have to carry babies within them for nine months, they can have hundreds of children if they can find enough women. And the way men did that was to steal women from other men through war: they killed the men and enslaved the women and turned them into baby-making machines. Of course, they were *men's* babies, and women had no rights over children because it was the man who reproduces, while women do not reproduce themselves and so have no reproductive rights.

This is why the change from a female-seed life view to a male-seed life view led humanity away from peaceful gender coexistence, and into the nightmare for women that we can still recognise today in patriarchal behaviour and attitudes.

One of the earliest Neolithic cultures were the Natufians who lived in Syria, Lebanon, Jordan, Palestine, and Israel between 12,500-9,000 BC. The Natufians started out as hunter gatherers. They hunted gazelle and deer, and gathered fruits, nuts, seeds, and wild grains such as barley and wheat. They invented the sickle, devised very effective storage facilities for the grain, and became a successful group. People had already started to domesticate animals, probably by taking the young of wild pigs, sheep, goats and cattle into their settlements. Dogs evolved in this way from wild wolves. Many groups settled in one place for part of the year and travelled around the rest. Some settled for a while and then returned to a nomadic lifestyle of hunting and gathering.

The Natufians provide us with the first clear Neolithic image of intercourse. Known as the Ain Sakhri figurine, it's a 10cm high sculpture formed from a calcite cobble showing a couple embracing in an upright position, their legs around each other. When the piece is turned upside down, we can see they're having sex. Experts at The British Museum, where this small sculpture is housed, make the point that the gender of one figure is unclear, leaving open the possibility this is a homosexual image.

If the Ain Sakhri figurine shows heterosexual sex, it tells us that intercourse may now have special significance in terms of reproduction. But to be sure of that interpretation, we have to wait until 6,000 BC when someone in Çatalhöyük in Turkey made a 4½ inch (11.6cm) high-relief carving in stone showing an embracing couple on the left, and a woman holding a child on the right, illustrating that embrace leads to babies.

Fig. 11. Çatalhöyük Group, Turkey, 6,000 BC, high-relief stone carving, 11.6cm high.

The question is, of course, what did people think was happening during intercourse? To answer this, we need to ask what kind of cultures these were. As we have seen, at Çatalhöyük women were associated with seed and, possibly, ancestral ties. The Natufians are thought to have been matrilocal, where men moved to the houses of their wives, and matrilineal, with descent and inheritance going along the female line. All that points to a female-seed life view, so early erotic images are likely depicting the male watering the female.

47: THE BLOOD-LINE

If women were perceived as the source of seed, the blood-line would pass through them and, indeed, it did. Descent and inheritance through the mother-daughter line was the practice in Ghana, Nubia, Libya, Ethiopia, Egypt, Palestine, Mesopotamia, Thrace, Anatolia, Persia, Crete, Etruria, India, Polynesia and, indeed, wherever there are records old enough to prove the point.

Civilisations that lasted for thousands of years, like Sumeria/Mesopotamia and Egypt, had their roots in a time when society was female-centered, then went through a transitional period, and ended as male-centered. Traditions that continue from earliest times are known as archaic. In Egypt, the archaic system of mother-kin lasted for thousands of years, with inheritance and property passing through the female line, even into Roman times – long after the male-seed, patriarchal life-view had taken hold. Egyptologist Barbara Lesko has written that:

"The importance of the mother in the Egyptian family is reflected in the literature of all periods as well as in the fact that Egyptian men, even those of the highest social class and in highest ranks of the civil service or the military, often placed only their mother's names on their monuments and other documents."

One of the original excavators of the pyramids, Sir Flinders Petrie, wrote:

"In Egypt all property went in the female line, the woman was the mistress of the house; and in early tales she is represented as having entire control of herself and the place. Even in late times the husband made over all his property and future earnings to his wife in his marriage settlement."

Lesko confirms the independence of women during the Old Kingdom, between 2,680 and 2,160 BC: "It would seem that few restrictions were placed on women of ability and high social status."

As the male-seed idea of reproduction took hold, and inheritance through the male line the common way of doing things, we arrived at a point where there were just a few societies left where the mother-daughter blood-line continued. These were curiosities to the earliest travel writers like the 5th century BC Herodotus who wrote, "Ask a Lycian who he is and he answers by giving his own name, that of his mother and so on in the female line." Lycia was a collection of city states on the south-western coast of Turkey. In the 4th century BC the Greek astronomer Heraclides Ponticus said of them "From days of old they have been ruled by women." And in the 1st century BC, the Greek Historian Nicolaus of Damascus said of the Lycians, "They name themselves after their mothers and their possessions pass by inheritance to the daughters instead of the sons."

Other places also followed the blood-line through females. In the 2nd century BC Polybius wrote of the Locrians, "(they) themselves have assured me that all nobility of ancestry among them is derived from women and not from men." In the 1st century BC, Diodorus Siculus wrote "... only the daughters inherit in Egypt," and around the same time the geographer Strabo said that among the Cantabrians inheritance was through the daughters who "had the obligation to supply their brothers with dowries." Strabo also reported that there was no such thing as an illegitimate child in Armenia because children took their names from their mothers.

There are people who find it hard to believe the bloodline went through females in ancient times. But in some places it still existed within living memory and we have witness accounts to prove it. Here, in the words of an old Nootka woman from Vancouver Island, Canada, is an account of how things were before the European invaders arrived, as recorded by Anne Cameron in *Daughters of Copper Woman*:

"'My grandmother was the Queen Mother,' she said suddenly and flatly, replacing her cup and picking up her knitting again. 'Her son was the king. She wasn't Queen Mother because he was the king, like in England. He was king only because she was Queen Mother. His son wouldn't inherit to be king. The Queen Mother's oldest girl, my mother, would become Queen Mother and her son – my brother – would have been king. I would have been Queen Mother after my mother because I was the oldest girl, and my son would have been king. Your mother, Ki-Ki, would have been Queen Mother, and if you'd had a brother, he'd have been King. Then you'd have been Queen Mother and your son would have been king.'

'Only it all got buggered', she amended calmly, flashing a funny twisted smile at Suzy and me. Got real buggered because the ships came and instead of chasin' them away because of what happened before, the people hoped this time things'd be different'."

Of course things were not different and the Europeans, with their patriarchal mind-set, took over the Native Americans' land. When they came to do 'land deals', it was often Native American women who came forward to sign the documents. This shocked the Europeans who had denied women any power and property rights for a couple of thousand years. At the time of the European invasions some Native American groups were patrilineal and others were matrilineal – such as the northeastern Naudenosaunee and the southwestern Navajo and Hopi.

SELECTED REFERENCES:
Lesko, Barbara S., *Biblical Archaeologist*, Vol.54, No.1, March 1991. This publication has been renamed *Near Eastern Archaeology Magazine* and is

published by the American Schools of Oriental Research at Boston University.
Petrie, William M. Flinders, Sir, *Egypt and Israel*, London: Society for Promoting Christian Knowledge, 1911, page 23.
Cameron, Anne, *Daughters of Copper Woman*, London: Women's Press, 1984, page 100.

48: THE EVOLUTION OF GODS

For all the evidence of gods and kingship during the early phase of human civilisation, the importance of the male shouldn't be over-estimated. Gerda Lerner observes that:

"At first, the tree of life, with its fruit – the cassia, the pomegranate, the date, the apple – was associated with fertility-goddesses. At the time of the development of kingship, kings assume some of the services to the goddess and with them some of her power, and have themselves depicted with symbols associated with her. They carry the water-of-life jug; they water the tree of life. It is most likely that this development coincided with the change in the concept of the fertility goddess: namely, that she must have a male consort to initiate her fertility. The king of the Sacred Marriage becomes the king 'watering' the tree of life."

In 1894 the Scottish Professor of Divinity William Robertson Smith had no idea that archaeologists over the next century or so would be excavating thousands of figurines in female form and setting off an argument about the existence, or not, of 'goddesses'. He relied on ancient Arabic and Hebrew texts to come to his conclusions in *Religion of The Semites*. In this book, he tells us that the existence of gods did not denote the concept of "fatherhood," and that the parent of "the stock" – the people – was originally thought to be female:

"... the history of the family render it in the highest degree improbable that the physical kinship between the god and his worshippers, of

which traces are found all over the Semitic area, was originally conceived as fatherhood. It was the mother's, not the father's blood which formed the original bond of kinship among the Semites as among other early peoples, and in this stage of society, if the tribal deity was thought of as the parent of the stock, a goddess, not a god, would necessarily have been the object of worship."

Gods have their own history. They first appear as the sons of parthenogenetic goddesses (women who reproduce on their own). In time, they become their mother's lovers, then their consorts and, in time again, they become deputies to the goddess – exercising power on her behalf. Later still, the myths tell us how gods usurped power from the goddesses, and we begin to see gods as the ultimate creative force. By this time, of course, the male-seed theory of life had taken hold.

SELECTED REFERENCES:
Lerner, Gerda, *The Creation of Patriarchy*, Oxford: Oxford University Press, 1986, page 195. By permission of Oxford University Press Inc. www.oup.com.
Smith, W. Robertson, *Lectures on the Religion of the Semites*, 2nd Ed., London: A. and C. Black, 1894, Lecture 2, pages 51-52. (Also known by the title *Religion of the Semites*).

49: LIBERATED WOMEN

Before 1869 in England and America, a married woman came under the legal doctrine called 'coverture' which meant that she was not, legally, a person. The husband and wife were considered, in law, one person – and that person was the husband. The wife couldn't own property, take out a mortgage, enter into any legal contracts, inherit money or land, or go into education. She could work, but the wages belonged to her husband.

This situation changed somewhat with the UK's Married Women's Property Act of 1870, which deemed she could keep her wages, and inherit property, and cash up to £200. However, she couldn't get back any property she inherited before marriage – that stayed with her husband. In 1935 the law changed again and married women could then sign legal documents and fully own property. In the 1960's though, most UK banks still wouldn't give a woman a mortgage. But at least she could have a bank account – which women in Lebanon couldn't get until 2009.

All this discrimination would have been shocking to ancient Egyptian women living during The New Kingdom, between 1,567-1,085 BC, according to Egyptologist Barbara Lesko:

"Numerous texts have survived from this period, including court documents and private letters revealing that women had their own independent legal identity on a par with men and that they could inherit or purchase property and dispose of it without a male co-signatory or legal guardian. Indeed, women were the heads of households, testified in court, witnessed documents, acted as executors of their family estates and assumed the obligations of a citizen vis-à-vis the State. Numerous records show this was true of free women in general, not just those of the gentry. On a personal level, it is clear that women enjoyed freedom of movement and association, that they could marry and divorce at will, that they engaged in commerce and that they were able to exercise authority over others in the work-place or temple."

According to 'the father of history', Herodotus, who travelled around Egypt in the 5th century BC, "Among them the women attend markets and traffic, but the men stay at home and weave." Four hundred years later, the intrepid Greek historian Diodorus Siculus was in Egypt and he wrote:

"It was ordained that the queen should have greater power and honour than the king and that among private persons the wife should enjoy authority over the husband, husbands agreeing in the marriage contract that they will be obedient in all things to their wives."

And this is the wording of the groom's pledge from a first century BC Egyptian marriage contract, as reported by Diodorus:

"I bow before your rights as wife. From this day on, I shall never oppose your claims with a single word. I recognise you before all others as my wife, though I do not have the right to say you must be mine, and only I am your husband and mate. You alone shall have the right of departure ... I cannot oppose your wish wherever you desire to go. I give you ... (a list of the bridegroom's possessions)."

In the neighbouring country of Libya, Diodorus found that:

"All authority was vested in the women, who discharged every kind of public duty. The men looked after the domestic affairs just as the women do among ourselves and did as they were told by their wives. They were not allowed to undertake war service or to exercise any functions of government, or to fill any public office, such as might have given them more spirit to set themselves up against women. The children were handed immediately after birth to the men, who reared them on milk and other foods suitable to their age."

He also reported "there have been in Libya a number of races of women who were warlike and greatly admired for their manly vigor." On the west coast of Turkey, Diodorus found that men carried out domestic duties, including the spinning of wool, while "women held the supreme power and royal authority." These people worshipped "The Mother of All Deities."

The indigenous people living in Greece before the violent Mycenaeans invaded in 1,500 BC, and the patriarchal Dorians in 1,200 BC, were called Pelasgians by the classical writers. Apparently men served the women in bed, at work in the fields, while hunting animals, and during war. Women were in charge. The early Greeks produced artefacts showing women leading the hunt, driving chariots, and directing proceedings in the courts of law.

What we have here are the echoes of a time when women

had complete freedom, and authority in society. But the fabric of those societies was unravelling and being rewoven in the male-seed pattern. Consequently, at this time, we see societies that appear paradoxical – partly female-centered but also partly male-centered. This is characteristic of a transitional phase, the interface between past and future. Think of women today – in some ways we're liberated, and in other ways we're not, and some places are more liberated than others. Change is never neat.

SELECTED REFERENCES:
Lesko, Barbara S., *Biblical Archaeologist*, Vol.54, No.1, March 1991. This publication has been renamed *Near Eastern Archaeology Magazine* and is published by the American Schools of Oriental Research at Boston University.

50: PATTERNS OF FEMALE POWER

It can be difficult to accept there was a time when women had more power than men because it's not something we're used to. So, before looking at the ancient past, it may help open our minds to that possibility by looking at more recent cultures where we've hard evidence for various patterns of female power.

One theme in history is where female power was behind a male 'front'. For example, the Ashanti warrior kings had to repel invaders from their gold-rich lands and were the active face of power in Ghana from the 1300's AD. However, that was a 'front' because the spiritual base of their power lay with the king's mother – the Queen Mother. She had final say in all matters, and her son became king only because he was her son. Things changed in the 1770's when King Osai Kojo consolidated a new unity of kingdoms by encouraging the appointment of men of ability, rather than men who wielded power only because they were their mother's sons.

The Iroquois (or Naudenosaunee) federation of Native Americans were a mother-centred, mother-right people. According to Paula Gunn Allen, their "political organisation was based on the central authority of the Matrons, the Mothers of the Longhouses (clans)". If a woman took her husband's name after marriage, she became ineligible for appointment to the Matron's Council.

When the European invaders landed in North America they only saw 'the red chief', because he and the warriors were the 'front' of tribal society. What was less obvious was that there was also a 'white chief,' as Allen explains:

"There is an old tradition among numerous tribes of a two-sided, complementary social structure. In the American Southeast this tradition was worked out in terms of the red chief and the white chief, positions held by women and by men and corresponding to internal affairs and external affairs. They were both spiritual and ritualistic, but the white chief or internal chief functioned in harmony-effective ways. This chief maintained peace and harmony among the people of the band, village, or tribe and administered domestic affairs. The red chief, also known as the war chief, presided over relations with other tribes and officiated over events that took people away from the village."

We can speculate that there were ancient societies in which power was held entirely by women because we can see it happening in modern times. Among the Minangkabau people of Bukittinggi, Sumatra, the westernmost island of Indonesia, the birth of a girl is a "blessed event" and grandma is the boss. Author Richard Mahler explains:

"The eldest living female in a family is considered the matriarch and has the most power in the household, which can number as many as 70 people, all descended from one ancestral mother and living under the same roof. She is deferred to in all matters of family politics."
"Property, though worked and used collectively, is passed on through the female line of the family, inherited by the daughters in the family.

All progeny from a marriage are regarded as part of the mother's family group and the father has little if any say in family matters."

And the matriarch has political power too:

"In the community at large, the eldest women in each family get together in large meeting houses to make decisions on a consensus basis. I'm not sure of the exact nature of the decisions they convene to discuss, although I assume they have to do with projects affecting all members of a village, such as water projects, schools and so on."

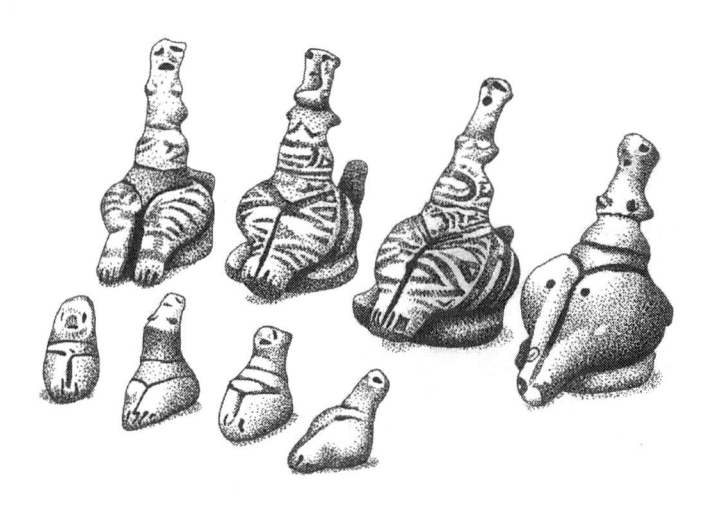

Fig. 12. The Assembly of Snake Goddesses 4,800-4,600 BC.
21 figurines ranging from 6-9cm high. Found stored in a large vessel at Poduri-Dealul Ghindaru, Romania.

That description reminds me of me of a collection of 21 little figurines, arranged within a vase, known as 'the assembly of snake goddesses' from Moldavia, in north-eastern Romania, dated around 4,700 BC **(Fig. 12)**. The collection consists of some highly decorated seated female figurines, some smaller undecorated figurines, and two small objects that might indicate this scene represents a ritual. It could depict young women being initiated into womanhood, or it could simply show a group of women talking, singing, chanting or whatever. In a sense, it doesn't matter what they're doing. Whatever it is, they're doing it together and, presumably, for the common good. And whatever they were doing, it was important enough to illustrate in three-dimensional form, and then hide in a vase for safekeeping.

SELECTED REFERENCES:
Allen, Paula Gunn, *The Sacred Hoop*, 1986, page 18. Copyright © 1986, 1992 by Paula Gunn Allen. Reprinted by permission of Beacon Press, Boston.
Mahler, Richard, *Great Expeditions*, (May-June 1991), page 21.

51: THE POWER BEHIND THE THRONE

In museums around the world we can see sculptures of ancient Egyptian kings, often with their wife and children shown on a smaller scale. This didn't mean the wife was inferior. On the contrary, as Egyptologist Barbara Lesko explains:

"The fact that the king's family were often depicted at the level of the legs of his colossal figure should not blind us to the importance of the great royal wife in Egyptian history. The queen was often of purer royal blood than her husband, whose claim to the throne she legitimised."

Many ancient texts and artefacts indicate there was a time when a man only became chieftain or king because he had an association with the source of power – a female. This means one thing – descent was in the female line, and it was the case in many ancient societies around the Mediterranean and elsewhere. 'Keeping it in the family', to ancient royalty, often meant incest – where a man marries a close female relative, particularly his sister, to acquire the throne. It would not be the son of such a marriage that inherits the throne. A daughter would be the heiress to the power, and the man who marries her could get access to the throne, and essentially rule on her behalf.

Going back even further in time, many archaeologists say

there were goddess religions and the priestess who officiated on her behalf, or the woman considered the matriarch of the tribe, was in total control of the society. Around her were 'male-satellites' – husband, lover, sons, or brothers. These men may have had status in society but it was only because they had an association with her.

The Sumerian goddess Inanna was represented on earth by a priestess who was the dominant partner in her relationship with the king. Apparently, kings did not make decisions on their own. Before doing anything hasty, he had to consult the priestess who, after some oracular divination and prophecy (consultation with the goddess), would give the instructions.

The king didn't appoint the chief priestess. She appointed him. According to Sumerian documents, he attained his position once he had 'proved himself' in her bed – that is, the bed of the goddess, represented by the priestess. The kings were mystically identified with Damuzi (the god), and were known as the 'beloved husbands' of Inanna.

In Iran, from 2,500 to 1,100 BC there was a kingdom called Elam. There, the goddess was called Anahita, and she gave the king authority, through her priestess, when she gave him 'the kingdom ring'.

During the Old Kingdom in Egypt, from 2,680 to 2,160 BC, women had more access to spiritual authority than they do now. And, according to Barbara Lesko:

"It is interesting to note that religious positions were not limited to noble-women, for we have found priestesses of major goddesses who bear humble titles such as tenant farmer. Many administrative, honorific and priestly titles for women have been recovered from Old Kingdom monuments ..."

Women had spiritual authority because they were more 'in likeness' to the goddess, and this ancient form of authority lingered well into the male-seed, and male-led, era. The male rulers still felt they needed the protection of the goddesses and were hedging their bets – paying homage to both male and female deities. As they became more confident in the idea of a male seed as the source of creation, the goddesses would be dropped.

The last vestiges of the female religions came in the form of advice through female prophetesses, who were thought to have a special link with goddesses, like the 'Pythian' at the oracle of Delphi. Male rulers went to her to get information and advice about the future, making the prophetess the last woman to have influence over affairs of state.

SELECTED REFERENCES:
Lesko, Barbara S., *Biblical Archaeologist*, Vol.54, No.1, March 1991. This publication has been renamed *Near Eastern Archaeology Magazine* and is published by the American Schools of Oriental Research at Boston University.

52: SEXUAL FREEDOM

When men think of themselves as 100% the source of human seed, the authors of creation, the patriarchs, there is one thing uppermost in their minds – female chastity. If a woman sleeps around, a man can't be sure whose seed is growing inside her womb. Paternity is uncertain. This is a logic women living in male-seed cultures also understand. They know that if they have sex with multiple partners, and get pregnant, they won't know whose child it is. Plus, of course, depending on where they live, they might get stoned to death. The patriarchal mind-set allows women no sexual freedom.

Today, in places liberated from the male-seed mind-set, men think of themselves as 50% the source of human seed. Women also think of themselves as the source of 50% of the human seed. We call it DNA – 23 chromosomes of which are contributed by each parent. Children, likewise, know they have two parents and even if the mother and father aren't living together, the child has the right to seek out the absent parent and make contact. Women today are free to have equal access to their children, to choose the man they want to share parentage with and even, if they can't find that man, go to a sperm bank and choose one from a catalogue. The equal-parentage mind-set gives women sexual freedom, but she is expected to be responsible and not confuse the paternity of a child by being promiscuous. Or, in the case of uncertainty, carry out DNA fingerprint testing so the paternity of a child can be established – for the child's sake, as well as for the father's.

Now imagine a mind-set where people think children are 100% the grown seed of the mothers. There are no fathers. If there's no father, allegiances are to the mother's family. If there's no father, it doesn't matter who mother sleeps with. If there's no father, no man is going to come along and say "that's my child, hand him over." If there's no father, a woman can sleep with ten men on the same day and, from a reproduction point of view, it doesn't matter. For women, that is total sexual freedom.

The degree of sexual freedom experienced by women is a clue to the reproduction theory of the people at that time and place. We know from the Old Testament in the Bible that the Jewish patriarchs were shocked and horrified by the loose sexual behaviour of people who worshipped 'idols' – particularly female idols related to the worship of 'the queen of heaven'. This in itself tells us that there were two standards of sexual behaviour in the one location, and two reproduction theories.

The earliest culture from which we have written evidence is Sumerian which spanned thousands of years and changed over that time. Religion was essentially local – each city having its own deities, and generally the pattern was of male gods taking over the functions of female goddesses. In the earliest period of Sumeria there was one deity, the goddess Nammu of the city of Eridu. She was said to have created everything on her own. Nammu was replaced by the earth goddess 'Ki' and the sky god 'An', and this pair were worshipped in various cities. What is interesting to us here is that when the annual 'sacred marriage' took place in religious ceremony between the king and 'goddess' (probably represented by a priestess) it was the goddess who took the sexual initiative and invited the king to become her 'husband.'

One of the most important deities of Sumeria was the goddess Inanna, and she was a wild role model. Not only did she rage wars with 'rivers of blood', she refused to marry, had a stream of young male partners, a 'lap of honey,' a 'boat of heaven' and a head of dishevelled hair. She represented perhaps the sexual freedom women once had, before female sexuality became the tool of men's reproduction.

A group of women living within Sumerian temple complexes were known as *qadistu* – which disapproving scholars translated as 'prostitutes.' But the word actually means 'sanctified women' or 'holy women', and they were free to marry or not. *Qadistu* were often from respectable families and, through their association with the temples, were trading extensively, and themselves owned property and land. Indeed, it was written in law that *qadistu* should inherit a portion of their fathers' property. Given respect in law, yet apparently also having sexual freedom within the goddess temples, this raises the question – were *qadistu* having sex with multiple partners to confuse the issue – to make the paternity of their children uncertain so men couldn't claim them as their own? Was this an echo of how things were in the wider society when the goddess ruled supreme?

The past can often be heard echoing within religion because religious practice changes more slowly than the society around it. In Christianity, for example, rites are performed today that are said to have their roots in activities carried out two thousand years ago. Likewise, practices that may have originated thousands of years before continued in Sumeria long after the male-seed idea came along.

Even during the patriarchal age there was a legacy of promiscuous female sex associated with goddess temples. As late as the 5th century BC, the Greek historian Herodotus writes about the "shameful custom" of the Babylonians insisting that every woman, once in her life, goes to the "precinct of Venus" and "consort with a stranger." Women of every class are "not allowed to return home till one of the strangers throws a silver coin into her lap, and takes her with him beyond the holy ground … When she has gone with him, and so satisfied the goddess, she returns home." This kind of activity does not constitute 'sexual freedom,' but it does make paternity uncertain and, as such, may reflect one aspect of goddess religions.

Goddess temples encouraged women to have sex with strangers long into the patriarchal age, throughout the Mediterranean: in North Africa; Sicily; Cyprus; Greece; Palestine; Lebanon; and Turkey. Even as late as the first century AD, according to the writer Lucian, women had sex with strangers at the temple of Aphrodite in Corinth, Greece, on the feast day of Adonis.

Ancient religious practices can continue for thousands of years, and that is what we might be seeing here – echoes of earlier times when goddess religions, faced with competition from male religions, started the 'tradition' of female sex with strangers. It may have been a deliberate ploy to weaken the father-child bond.

Laws change with the times – slowly, and sometimes very slowly, but inevitably. One of the earlier Sumerian laws, at 2,370 BC, is known as The Code of Urukagina – and this included a 'reform' to abolish polyandry – the practice of a woman having several husbands. Clearly, if a woman has several sexual partners at the same time, no man can claim her children as his own.

Six hundred years later, in the Code of Hammurabi (137), the language is of women who "bore him children" and "provided him with children." In law 129, if a wife is caught in the act of having sex with another man, her fate is dependent on whether "the wife's master allows his wife to live." This is clearly the language of patriarchy although, unlike later cultures, the Mesopotamians were quick to kill a man found guilty of rape (Ur-Namma 6; Hammurabi 130; Middle Assyrian A12).

In the 5th century BC, Herodotus found pockets of promiscuity in places where it certainly wouldn't be allowed today. In Libya, for example, he found the Gindanes women displaying collections of leather ankle bands, each given to them by different sexual partners. He says "she who can show the most is the best esteemed, as she appears to have been loved by the greatest number of men." I wonder what reproduction theory the Gindanes had because it certainly doesn't sound like they thought along male-seed lines.

SELECTED REFERENCES:
Wink, Walter, *Engaging the Powers*, Minneapolis: Fortress Press, 1992, page 40.
Herodotus, *History of Herodotus*, Book 1 - 199 (Babylon); Book 4 (Gindanes).
Roth, Martha T, *Law Collections from Mesopotamia and Asia Minor*, Atlanta: Scholar's Press, 1995.

53: THE SACRIFICIAL KING

Female-seed religions thought the seed of life was in the woman and needed 'water' to make it germinate and grow. This was 'the sacred marriage', the basic act that promoted all life. Over the millennia, this sacred marriage took many different ritualistic forms, evolving with time.

Imagine the scene: a stage has been built high up and in view of all the people; the high priestess (representing the goddess) comes along with her young lover (representing the god). He'd been chosen for this role a year previously, since when he had enjoyed a life of luxury in the temple. The priestess and the young 'king' have sex in front of all the people, who probably also have sex. If a woman had sex with a man who was not her regular partner, or with multiple partners, and became pregnant on this festive day, the paternity of the child would be unknown.

But 'the annual king' was temporary and disposable. He had no seed and, consequently, no offspring. He'd done his job, and as if to illustrate the point, he was dispensed with. He was killed. There are many versions of 'the sacred marriage,' from Crete, Cyprus, Greece, Palestine, Syria, Carthage, Egypt, Sumer, Babylon, Zimbabwe, Nigeria, and Ireland. The 'king' was burnt alive, decapitated, strangled, or in various ways 'accidentally' killed.

'The sacred marriage', also known as *hieros gamos*, symbolised fertility of the earth. The ritual may have come about because vegetation goes through a fallow period so after the harvest or the autumnal fall, life seems dead. But hidden deep within the earth or plant, the seeds of life are waiting for the revival. Before the new growth there has to be a fallow period, a vegetation death. That's where 'the sacrificial king' came in or, perhaps more accurately, went out. His death symbolised the fallow period and was a sacrifice for the good of the whole community, so there would be a re-birth of vegetation and, given the orgiastic nature of the festivities, a re-birth of babies as well.

As time went on, the annual event changed so the year became 'the longer year' and, eventually, 'the annual king' became long term kingship. The king became a substitute for the god. In some places the king was prepared by various rituals so he became elevated to a god-like status. In others, he was symbolically fused with a fertility god. In all examples that we know of, however, it was the goddess who invited the king to her bed. She was in charge. Probably 'she' was the chief priestess, representing the goddess.

As time went on, the god-like king could no longer be killed off and substitutes for him had to be offered – other human beings, animals, or effigies like the 'mannequins' the Vestal Virgins threw into the Tiber River in Rome to 'drown'. Also, in some places, the death of the king was replaced by his humiliation – he was stripped, slapped, and thrown in the river, or had his head shaven and made to walk around in rags. One Babylonian tablet says that if the king doesn't cry when slapped, the omen is bad for the coming year.

In this tradition of punishing the king we see the priestess asserting her authority over the king. He has to cry so everyone can see he is sorry, and knows his place. Men were coming to think of themselves as the source of seed, and these old goddess traditions were a way to remind them of who was still, spiritually, in charge. If men challenged the reproductive status quo maybe the harvest would fail, everyone would starve ... and it would be the men's fault for being so arrogant as to think they had the seed. Men couldn't prove they had the seed, and so far the goddess religions had served the people well. The priestesses, and women in general, probably weren't keen for men to take control.

SELECTED REFERENCES:
Frankfort, Henri, *Kingship and the Gods*, Chicago: The University of Chicago Press (Phoenix Edition), 1978, pages 296-7.

54: WOMAN THE INVENTOR

Before women were imprisoned by men – intellectually as well as domestically – they were free to improve their lives in any way they saw fit and, with children to feed, they had plenty of incentive to do so. The most important discovery in human history was that the grain being collected for food was also seed that could be planted – and grown to provide more food. If contemporary hunter-gatherers provide clues to the behaviour of ancient hunter-gatherers, the likelihood is that women invented farming because it is usually women who gather food, and would have made the discovery that grain = seed.

The domestication of animals could also have been a female initiative. Although popular culture might depict the tough, strong hunter dominating an animal into submission, the easier route to animal domestication involves capturing an infant, perhaps after killing the mother, and rearing that infant back at the homestead. In Papua New Guinea, women suckle wild piglets at their breasts and in this way the animal is integrated into the household.

The Sumerian civilisation started around 5,000 BC with the cities of Eridu and Uruk and ran for almost 3,000 years before it became part of a greater area, known as Mesopotamia, which included land to the north (all in present day Iraq) and ran for another 1,000 years or so. Over that vast period of time, much changed. In the early days, goddesses were said to be responsible for all kinds of skills and crafts – while there were no corresponding male gods, but these skills later came to be identified with men and gods. For example: the goddess Ninurra looked after pottery; Ninmug was responsible for woodwork and metallurgy; Uttu for weaving; and Ninzadim for jewellery-making. It has been suggested that this change from female to male indicates that women carried out the skill activities first – which means they could have invented them. Later, as cities developed and people took on specialist jobs, men took the skills over, and male gods then became the protectors of these activities.

All over the ancient civilised world, people attributed the invention of writing to females: Isis was said to have given the alphabet to the Egyptians; the Hindu goddess of knowledge, Sarasvati, was thought to have invented the original alphabet; while Kali was said to have invented Sanskrit. Legend has it that Medusa gave the alphabet to Hercules, and that Carmenta created Latin from the Greek. The ancient Celts worshipped Brigit as the patron deity of language while the goddess Cerriwed was the source of intelligence and knowledge.

The first substantial examples of writing come from a temple built for the Sumerian goddess Inanna in a city called Uruk. The clay tablets with cuneiform writing are dated around 3,200 BC. At this time in history, temples were the centre of everything, not just religious matters. The land belonged to the goddess, and the priestesses and priests acted on her behalf, renting out land, and collecting in produce – fruit, vegetables, fish, animals, oil, nuts, and so forth. And people had to be paid. There was a massive amount of accounting to be done, and this is what the first tablets were about: record keeping.

A large group of priestesses living at the temples were known as *naditu*. They were from royal or well-to-do families, financially independent because they had a dowry from their family, owned their own homes, took out contracts, borrowed money, and carried out business. The word *naditu* means 'fallow,' because they were not expected to have children, and instead dedicated themselves to the work of the goddess. It's known that many *naditu* could write and, as 'necessity is the mother of invention', it's quite likely that it was one of them who invented writing, to keep an inventory of the goddess' assets.

The Sumerians themselves said the goddess Nidaba (or Nisaba) invented clay tablets and writing, and she was known as 'the learned one of the holy chambers. She who teaches the decrees, the great scribe of heaven.' Nidaba was also a goddess of Uruk so it seems likely she 'worked' through a particularly inventive priestess whose job it was to keep track of the vast temple estates.

In the Sumerian city of Ur in 2,354 BC, the priestess at the temple of Inanna was En Hedu'Anna – which means priestess (En), and 'ornament of heaven'. Although we don't know her birth name, Hedu'Anna produced the first literary works we can attribute to a particular person. There are over forty 'hymns' to the goddess Innana, and because so many copies were produced, the many broken bits of clay tablets can be put together so we have a good idea of what she wrote. This was the first mass-produced literature. But Hedu'Anna's main role was as chief astronomer of the moon goddess Nanna. She would have overseen the temple observatory and recorded the movements of planets and stars. Her father was King Sargon 1, who joined north and south Iraq, and En Hedu'Anna had an important role in blending into one religion the worship of the northern Akkadian goddess Ishtar with the southerly Sumerian goddess Inanna. This makes her the first known 'religious diplomat.'

In Egypt, the goddess of writing was Seshat, which was not a name as such but a description – 'female scribe'. No temples to her have been found but there were many priestesses dedicated to her, as well as a few priests. Seshat is shown wearing a panther-skin dress and with a seven-pointed emblem above her head. As well as being goddess of writing, she was goddess of architecture, mathematics, measurement, history, and accounting. She was linked to the goddesses Isis and Nephthys – who was called 'Seshat, Foremost of Builders' in texts found in pyramids. When the foundations of temples were being laid out, Seshat's chief priestess would accompany the Pharaoh in stretching the measuring cords and pegging out the axis, according to the stars. Her role was appropriated by the god Thoth, and Seshat was in later times shown with his symbol – a crescent moon, or horns, above her head. Sheshat lost her independence over time, becoming known as the daughter or wife of Thoth. Many other goddesses would be subject to such take-overs.

In India, there were notable female philosophers who engaged in the big questions: how did the universe originate; what is the soul; how does a person achieve immortality? In the first millennium BC these included Maitreyi, Gargi Vacknavi, and Lopamudar. All three were related in some way to male philosophers and it shows that women at this time needed the protection of men to indulge their passion for intellectual debate.

Until the 20th century, most women in Britain weren't given access to schools where they could learn, among other things, Pythagorean theory. But, ironically, Pythagoras himself was taught by a woman, Themistoclea, and married to an accomplished mathematician, Theano. She was thirty-six years younger than him; they had five children; and when he died she and her daughters, Damo, Arignote, and Myla, kept the school of Pythagorean thought going. They lived in Greek cities in southern Italy in the mid-sixth century BC, and were constrained in what they were allowed to do, as women. Although they could discuss the inherent mathematical order in the universe, they were prisoners of their time. And it was to get worse. In Athens, a hundred years later, women had no independence from men – it was forbidden by law.

When Egypt was under Roman rule, a woman called Hypatia taught mathematics and astronomy in Alexandria. She is said to have invented the planisphere, an astrological device; a hydroscope, or water clock; and an aerometer, an instrument for measuring the weight or density of air and gases. She was a brilliant teacher, unmarried, virtuous, and dignified, and students came great distances to gain the benefit of her knowledge. She is described as a 'pagan,' but we have no better description than that of her religious views. Certainly they didn't agree with those of the Christian mob who in 415 AD dragged her from her chariot, stripped her naked, and sliced the flesh from her body with sharpened flints and shells. There's some argument as to whether she was dead or alive when they burnt her body. Supposedly, the reason for this treatment was that she'd caused an argument between the Roman and Christian leaders, but that was a false allegation. More likely, brainy and independent-minded women couldn't be tolerated.

55: WHO WAS THE GODDESS?

It's difficult to imagine the mind-set of people who thought a female god was the source of everything in the universe, in just the same way as Judaism, Christianity, and Islam recognise a male creator who made everything in the universe, and every living thing in it, including us. But if people thought females were the only source of human life or, later, the human seed, they'd expect a female to be the source of everything else they could see. That would be logical.

People who actually worship a divine female creativity do not restrict that creativity to having babies, or helping plants grow. There is more to goddesses than 'fertility' – that ill-defined and therefore meaningless term. In the second century AD, the Roman writer Apuleius wrote *The Golden Ass*, in which the goddess Isis spoke:

"I am Nature, the universal Mother, mistress of all the elements, primordial child of time, sovereign of all things spiritual, queen of the dead, queen also of the immortals, the single manifestation of all gods and goddesses that are. My nod governs the shining heights of Heaven, the wholesome sea breezes, the lamentable silences of the world below. Though I am worshipped in many aspects, known by countless names and propitiated with all manner of different rites, yet the whole round earth venerates me."

The Lalita sahasranama is a sacred Hindu text recited today by worshippers of Devi, also known as Shakti, the Divine Mother, and consort of Shiva. This couple have gone through their own history, and through time Shiva has become more important than he once was. The Lalita sahasranama may have its roots in earlier times and it consists of one thousand 'names' or characteristics of the goddess. Number 295 describes her as "She who is mother of the world," but my favourite is number 620 - "She who is the mother of several billions of universes."

In East Asia, the Great Goddess is known as Mago in Korea, Magu in China, and Mako in Japan. According to Korean sources, female cosmic music brought Mago into being, along with the earth and stars. She gave birth parthenogenetically to two daughters, who each gave birth to two daughters and two sons – the first males.

In 1926 the German ethnologist Konrad Theodor Preuss published his conversations with the Kagaba people of Columbia, South America. These were translated by Paul Radin and show that the concept of 'a universal mother' was deeply embedded in the Kagaba cosmology:

"The mother of our songs, the mother of all our seed, bore us in the beginning of things and so she is the mother of all types of men, the mother of all nations. She is mother of the thunder, the mother of the streams, the mother of the trees and of all things. She is the mother of the world and of the older brothers, the stone-people. She is the mother of the fruits of the earth and of all things ... She alone is the mother of the fire and the Sun and the Milky Way ... She is the mother of the rain and the only mother we possess. And she has left us a token in all the temples ... in the form of songs and dances ... we think of the one and only mother of the growing things, of the mother of all things ... Our mother of the growing fields, our mother of the streams, will have pity upon us. For to whom do we belong? Whose seeds are we? To our mother alone do we belong."

Of Native North American spiritual concepts, Paula Gunn Allen states that although "contemporary Indian tales suggest that the creatures are born from the mating of sky father and earth mother," there are "older, more secret texts." Before the male revisions, which Allen says may have predated Christianity or occurred since its influence, there was 'Thought Woman.' This supreme spirit brought forth everything in the world through the act of thinking, or creating, it into being. Although a 'she,' Thought Woman is without gender in that she is both mother and father to all people and animals. Everything in the world is due to Thought Woman's powerful imagination – from physical skills such as farming, building and creativity, to innate human characteristics such as intuition, memory and language.

In our culture, when the word 'goddess' is used, it's usually prefixed with the words 'fertility' or 'mother.' This limits the scope of the goddess and denies the many other aspects that are, and have been, and probably were, attributed to her: bringer of death and regeneration/reincarnation; law-maker; prophetess; inventor; healer and warrior. Far from being the nice soothing mummy we can run to when in danger, in her association with carrion eating birds and animals the goddess was often portrayed as danger itself.

One long-running goddess theme is her association with large wild cats – felines. The oldest site of communal spiritual activity is Göbekli Tepe in eastern Turkey dated from 9,500 BC where the engraved image of a female was placed between two pillars decorated with lions. Two thousand years later the enthroned goddess from Çatalhöyük rests her hands on the heads of two leopards on either side of her. A seal dated around 4,000 BC from the Sarasvati-Indus civilisation shows a goddess with arms outstretched holding two felines – probably tigers – by their necks. She may have been an early incarnation of the goddess Durga who has been depicted riding on a feline – often a tiger – for many centuries, right up to the present time. The Iranian goddess Anahita is shown holding the front legs of two standing felines; while the Hittite goddess Hebat is shown either seated on a lion or, like the Hurrian goddess Shaushga, standing on a lion. The Egyptian goddess Qetesh is shown standing on a lion, as is the Sumerian goddess Inanna, and the Canaanite 'queen of heaven' Astarte. In Minoan images the goddess is shown on a mountain with two lions looking up at her, and in later times when she was known as Rhea, is depicted flanked by two lions, or riding a chariot pulled by lions. Mycenean seals show the goddess again flanked by two lions. The Greek goddess Cybele is shown seated between two lions or in a chariot being pulled by lions – with examples being uncovered from as far away as northern Afghanistan. Freyja is the name of the Norse goddess who rides a chariot drawn by two large felines.

In many cases the names of the goddesses are interchangeable, being called different names in different locations and times. And no doubt they had different meanings to the people who worshipped them. But the long time frame and diverse locations of this feline iconography begs the question: are we looking at the longest running spiritual theme?

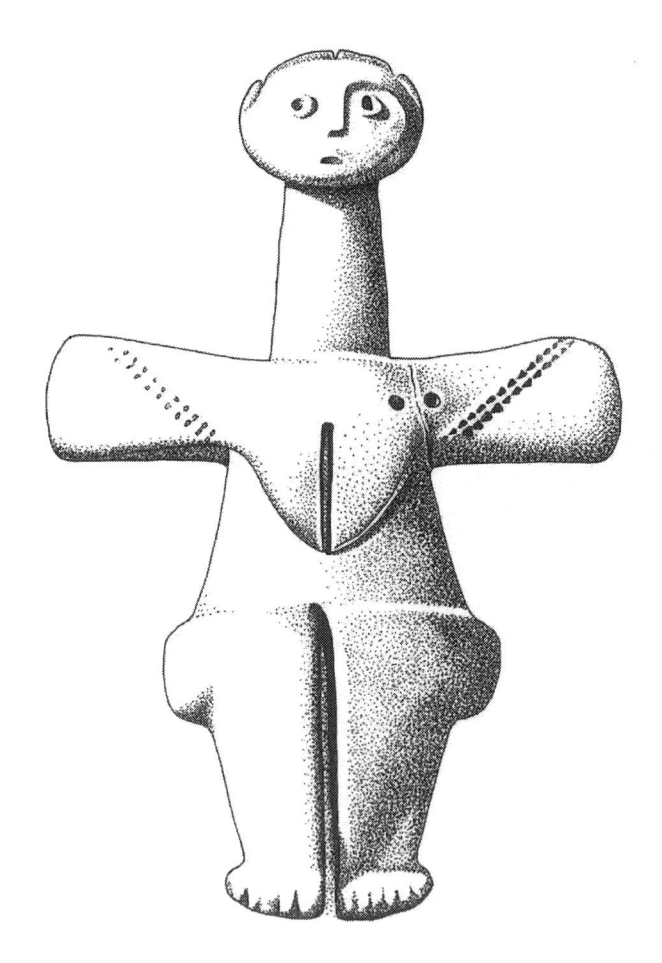

Fig. 13. Cyprus Goddess 3,000 BC, limestone, 39cm (15 inches) high.

Fig. 14. The Lady of Pazardzik 4,500 BC,
clay figurine, 15cm (6 inches) high, Bulgaria.

Because people talk about "fertility goddesses," you'd expect, perhaps, to find female figurines either pregnant, giving birth or holding a baby. But the vast majority are not. It's much more common to find goddess figurines holding serpents, lights, flowers, swords, bows and arrows. Elise Baumgartel, who excavated many early Egyptian sites writes "No figure of a woman with child ... is known to me from predynastic Egypt."

On the Cycladic islands in the Aegean Sea off Greece, between 5,000 and 2,400 BC, people sculpted beautiful little white figurines which both men and women took to their graves. The vast majority of the figurines are female yet few show any signs of pregnancy. Surely, if these female figurines were meant to indicate a 'fertility' goddess or a 'mother' goddess, they would be carrying babies in this life rather than being associated with the afterlife?

Some people think the female figurines were used in sympathetic magic rituals, particularly as requests to the 'fertility goddess' to make individual women pregnant. However, in ethnographic examples that we know of today, women are more likely to use a model of the desired for child. The first Egyptian figurine holding a child is dated around 2,120 BC, after the invention of writing and, indeed, a woman has written on it her desire for a child. So why shouldn't earlier figurines also show the baby? Or at least show the woman pregnant or giving birth? And if the prehistoric figurines show the desired-for-child grown up, why was the desired gender so often female?

Figurines without arms were common, and of the ancient Egyptian variety, Baumgartel wrote:

"It has been suggested that the female statuettes were concubines for the dead; but they were found with women even more frequently than with men, which seems to dispose of this suggestion. They also have been explained as servant-figures but servants without arms seems to defeat their own purpose."

Funny, isn't it, how anything female is assumed to be a 'servant' or a 'concubine' or, as some archaeologists seem to think, an early version of pornography made by men for their sexual satisfaction. More recently it's been suggested the figurines represent a goddess who was 'protector of the hearth', which is fine except that, again, this limits the goddess to the place in which the patriarchal male wanted to imprison women – at home. And to associate the goddess with 'fertility,' and even 'earth mother,' again limits the image of woman to a fertile mother – the creature the patriarchal male created, his baby-making machine. What's happening with all these descriptions is that the goddess is being limited to areas where women, in the patriarchal male-seed era, were confined. There seems to be a patriarchal veil of prejudice preventing the goddesses being seen as the source of wisdom, magic, fate, inspiration, change, and spirituality – none of which need have anything to do with having babies, or making plants grow. Yes, women have babies, but that's not *all* they do, or are.

We have thousands of female figurines to decipher. They weren't all goddesses. Some represented priestesses. Some may have represented female ancestors. Many were votive offerings – an item that expresses a wish, or a promise, or both, to the goddess. Some were found in shrines and on altars, or under the floors of temples. Some were put in graves – perhaps a symbol of the goddess was put there to protect the dead person on their journey into the afterlife. Some were found in the walls or under the floors of homes, and it's been suggested they were there to 'protect the home.' But, like images of Jesus found in homes around the world today, they probably meant much more than 'protector of the home.' Some figurines are found in rubbish pits, and it's been suggested the figurine represented the goddess absorbing an illness someone was suffering, then being smashed deliberately, as if to break the spell of disease.

When the Israelite tribes came into Canaan, they found the people there worshipping goddesses such as 'the queen of heaven,' and when the Torah and Bible talk about 'false gods' and 'idols,' it's female figurines they're usually talking about. The Israelites didn't need to ask 'who was the goddess?' They knew who she was – she was their number one enemy. And the three monotheistic patriarchal religions of Judaism, Christianity, and Islam would spend many centuries trying to wipe her, and her memory, off the spiritual landscape.

SELECTED REFERENCES:
Radin, Paul, *Monotheism among Primitive Peoples*, New York: Bollingen Foundation Special Publication No.4, 1954. Copyright © Bollingen Foundation and Princeton University Press.
Allen, Paula Gunn, *The Sacred Hoop*, 1986. Copyright © 1986, 1992 by Paula Gunn Allen. Reprinted by permission of Beacon Press, Boston, page 15.
Baumgartel, Elise J., *The Cultures of Prehistoric Egypt*, 1960, page 71. Published on behalf of the Griffith Institute, Ashmolean Museum, Oxford, by Oxford University Press. Copyright © Griffith Institute, University of Oxford.

FURTHER READING:
Lesko, Barbara S., *The Great Goddesses of Egypt*, Oklahoma: University of Oklahoma Press, 1999.
Goodison, Lucy, and Morris, Christine (Eds.), *Ancient Goddesses*, London: British Museum Press, 1998.

56: THE HISTORY OF THE PHALLUS

When we look at an image of a penis it can mean, reproductively speaking, four things. Working back in time, these are:

1. (1900 AD to now) Two seeds and fusion; the penis represents the delivery of sperm – 50% of the genetic material.

2. (3,000 BC to 1900 AD) In the male-seed era, the patriarchal age, the penis represented the delivery of the human seed – 100% of the genetic material.

3. (10,000 BC to 3,000 BC) In the female-seed era, the penis represented the delivery of water to irrigate the seed inside the woman – and contributed 0% of the genetic material.

4. (Before 10,000 BC) In the parthenogenetic-woman era the penis represented, perhaps, keeping the vagina open so the baby can come out or, simply, the sexual energy of men – and contributed 0% of the genetic material.

Because images of the phallus are rare until 10,000 BC, archaeologists have often made a distinction between 4 and 3, saying that 'men discovered their role in reproduction' around 10,000 BC. This is wrong by about 12,000 years, because men discovered their true role in reproduction around the turn of the 20th century AD. But there certainly was a big change in 10,000 BC – when men started to have a role in reproduction, even if it was just a peripheral role, as waterer. For them, this was a big step forward.

Because of the very widely held notion that 'people have always known the facts of life,' images of the penis created during eras 1-3 have been interpreted as having more or less the same meaning. Nothing could be further from the truth. We're currently engaged in a 'battle of the sexes' while we switch from phallic eras 2 to 1, and women all over the world are trying to regain control over their lives. This battle means a switch for men from 100% to 50% control over the reproductive process, and for women it's a switch from 0% to 50%. But this battle is nothing compared to the battle that took place on the interface between eras 3 and 2, when it was either 100% the woman's baby, or 100% the man's. That switch, from female-seed culture to male-seed culture happened over a very long period of time, each culture having its own experience of the battle.

One culture that seemed to suddenly disappear developed on the small islands of Malta and nearby Gozo in the Mediterranean between around 5,000 to 2,500 BC. At its longest point, Malta is only 27 km long, yet in this small area archaeologists have found 23 temples. They have a distinct design, often compared to the vagina and womb of a woman's body. The entrance is a trilithon (2 vertical stones that support a horizontal stone on top) behind which is a passage leading to a large oval-shaped chamber and, often, another passage leading to one or more chambers. It seems the idea behind these temples was that the community could, symbolically, enter the body of the goddess and, after some kind of ritual, leave in some sense reborn. Maltese expert J. Bezzina here explains the locations in which the phallus was found:

"The phallic symbol was introduced in the last part of the temple period, though it never gained a place in the 'Holy of Holies' where the goddess was dominant. It was found either outside the temple in a deliberately built up niche, in the exterior wall (Hagar Qim) or in the interior, facing the Holy of Holies (Tarxien) or in one of the apses near the sacred place. In all cases it is facing a downward-tapering slab or

the Pubic Triangle, thought to represent the female. From these symbols it is understood that fertility was very much involved."

In this fertility the male role was secondary, not central. Although some very impressive female sculptures have been found, the Maltese style of depicting humans was that they were very fat, and clothed, which makes it hard to be certain of the gender of many other artefacts. Another interesting feature of this culture is a series of egg or womb-shaped underground chambers (a hypogeum) at Hal Saflieni, made between 4,000-2,500 BC.

One culture that seems to have made a slow transition from female-centred to male-centred is the Sarasvati-Indus civilisation that, from 7,000 to 1,900 BC, covered a massive area, 2000 miles long and 800 miles wide, in present day western Pakistan and India. It's named after the two rivers along which 1,400 sites have been found. The earliest settlement uncovered so far, dated 7,000-2,600 BC, is Mehrgarh. There, all human figurines were made in the form of females until 4,000 BC, after which male figurines were also increasingly made.

Later sites include Mohenjo-daro, a city built on a grid system and housing 40,000 people. Each house had its own bathroom and toilet, which were connected to a public drainage system, and there was also a 'Great Bath,' about 30 x 25 feet (9 x 8 meters) in size, probably used for ritual purposes. There were no huge temples so archaeologists think people worshipped at small shrines in their own homes.

Another city in this culture was Harrapa, which was inhabited from 3,300 to 1,300 BC. Much of the site still needs to be excavated but it has already revealed many human figurines, mostly big-breasted females. One shows a female with another incomplete body – just the buttocks and thighs – entwined with her in a lover's embrace. The Sarasvati-Indus civilisation produced seals that appear to show both male and female deities. One image is very recognisable as the male god Shiva but other seals show females in dominant roles, for example a goddess standing in an arch made of leaves from the pipal tree, with a male kneeling down to her.

There has been quite a lot of argument among archaeologists about whether some artefacts from this civilisation are linga and yoni. These are representations of the phallus and vulva, which can be seen in intimate combination today in innumerable temples, in India and elsewhere. Conical stones are said by some to represent linga but others say they are objects for games. Also, there are circular stones with holes in them, said to represent yoni, but they are not found in close connection with stones that could be linga. However, there is one late Harappan object, which looks exactly like the lingam and yoni combination you can find in art, in temples, in homes, and in fact everywhere in India – the symbol of Shiva and the goddess Shakti.

For many reasons, there seems to be a continuity of symbolism from the earliest period of Indian history, right up to date. However, the meaning of the lingam – the phallus – has undoubtedly changed over that time. The male wasn't represented at all to begin with; then we increasingly see more male figurines; then both female goddesses and male gods on seals; and eventually – as we enter the male-seed era – stories begin to tell us that Shiva's lingam grew so enormous, it reached from the upper stratosphere to the core of the earth. By this time of course the phallus had become the tool that delivered the male seed into the female soil.

In ancient Egypt there was a god called Min who was responsible for the fertility of plants and animals. He is always shown with an erect penis. In later times he represented the delivery of semen but from the earliest times he was known as the 'opener of clouds' – the rain-maker, the waterer. Min was mentioned in the tombs of the Old Kingdom in the 3rd millennium BC. He originated in 'Upper Egypt,' which is the southern part of Egypt, near present day Sudan, which was joined with 'Lower Egypt' in 3,100 BC. Africa had a very ancient tradition of 'rainmaker-kings,' and a veneration for cattle. In the so-called 'Palette of Narmer' – which commemorated the union of Upper and Lower Egypt – the cow-goddess Hathor is shown on both sides, and the goddess Sekhmet is prominent, as 2 lionesses, on one side. All this adds up to a time when goddesses were paramount, and when men were associated primarily with water. In later times, the Egyptians were keen to dismiss females from the creative process, to the extent that they imagined the sun god Amun Ra creating the world through masturbation.

Fig. 15. Avenue of Priapus, Delos, Greece. 3rd century BC.
Reconstruction of avenue of columns with carved phalluses.

On the Greek island of Delos you can see the remains of a third century BC avenue comprised of pillars, on top of which were huge stone phalluses **(Fig. 15).** These celebrate the cult of the god Priapus, who was always shown with a huge erect penis. Apparently, Roman women would sit on smaller versions of Priapus' penis, in the hope it would help them become pregnant.

In Japan, until a few decades ago, farming communities held fertility dances around a giant phallus made of straw, then it would be put on a cart which everyone would follow to a field where the phallus was burnt in offering to the sun, so it might return again. Today, the phallus as fertility object is extravagantly displayed in Shinto shrines. Dozens of huge upstanding phalluses, usually made of wood, recognise the reproductive man. There is also usually a single Torii arch – emblem of the female aspect. These temples are often set in beautiful gardens and couples hoping for a child can spend the night there.

The mystery of life has always been associated with religious and spiritual matters. But a phallus, on its own, tells us nothing unless we understand the historical context. The contemporary Japanese Shinto shrines are expressions of the male-seed history which, although now superseded by scientific facts, still echoes in 'tradition.' In every archaeological context, we need to question "is that phallus providing water, or seed?"

But a penis is also about sex, intercourse, pleasure, and the unity of opposites. And that side of life needs to be put into the discussion as well, which makes this subject even more complex. The discovery of an ancient phallus should not lead to that phrase I have heard so often – "men now understood their role in reproduction." In fact, men only understood their actual role around the turn of the 20th century AD. Before then, it was one misconception after another. Understanding those misconceptions helps us to understand those cultures.

SELECTED REFERENCES:
Bezzina, J., *The Ggantija Temples*, Gozo, Malta: Xaghra, 2002, page 4.

PART FOUR: THE TAKE-OVER

57: THE TAKE-OVER

An idea can change the world. And it did. When men began to think they were the source of the singular seed it was a profound revolution and many battles would be fought over it. This was what was at stake:

\multicolumn{2}{FEMALE SEED}	\multicolumn{2}{MALE SEED}
FOR WOMEN	FOR MEN	FOR WOMEN	FOR MEN
Children are hers	Has no children	Has no children	Children are his
Female ancestors	Female ancestors	Male ancestors	Male ancestors
Deity is female	Deity not male	Deity not female	Deity is male
Spiritual authority	No spiritual authority	No spiritual authority	Spiritual authority
Inherits land	Does not inherit land	Does not inherit land	Inherits land

When the male-seed idea came along it gave men authority they had not experienced before. But, on top of that, it introduced a concept people had not known up to this point – the need for one person, the male, to control the means of his reproduction, the female.

FEMALE-SEED LIFE-VIEW	She has the seed. She has the means of production (womb). **She does not need to control the male.**
MALE-SEED LIFE-VIEW	He has the seed. He does not have the means of production. **He has to control the means of production - the female.**

The difference between the idea of a female-centred creativity and a male-centred one is simply that – an idea. Nobody could prove the point either way. Both ideas were wrong but, at the same time, both ideas were right: the seed *is* in the woman and the seed *is* in the man. The problem was that nobody knew about two seeds and fusion so nobody could be 100% right. What they did know is that a single seed has the potential for life, and future generations of life. Arguments were inevitable.

In parts of the world that developed farming, the male-seed idea seems to have started around 3,000 BC. This is about the time the plough was invented and you can almost picture the scene: a man is ploughing all day, up and down the field, day in day out, looking down at the furrow he's cut into the earth. He throws seed into the shallow trench and has a thought: "This furrow looks like a vulva, and when I ejaculate into my wife's vulva, maybe I'm planting seed in her."

That's all it would take to cause a revolution, especially if a lot of men had the same idea at the same time. But before the revolution could happen men had to get the idea accepted by the women in their lives, and that wasn't going to be easy. Not only was there mother to consider, and the wife, all the other women in the village, and the priestess, there was the goddess who presided over everyone, and gave them her protection. Arguing the case was a gamble, especially when you had no proof.

In parts of the world where there was no farming, and only

a nomadic way of life following herds of animals, the idea of male generativity could have developed from the simple idea of 'no ram=no lamb.' Watching animals all day, and trying to encourage them to multiply, can easily lead to the idea that the male impregnates not just one, but many females of the herd. It is not an inevitable consequence of keeping animals, especially when you already have other ideas of reproduction that you project onto your animals, but it can be a consequence. And it seems it was the idea that developed on the vast Eurasian steppes, because pastoral and patriarchal people from that area invaded the matriarchal cultures of Europe, and took over. A revolution certainly occurred, as here described by Amaury de Riencourt:

"It is in the amazing metamorphosis of the old matriarchal mythologies that the depth and importance of this profound psychological revolution can be best understood. All the mythologies were taken over and stood on their head; all the female-oriented myths were reinterpreted patriarchally. What had been good became bad, former heroes became demons, and the remarkable coincidence was that this metamorphosis happened more or less simultaneously, over a period of time, in the Indo-European and Semitic worlds, in Greece as in India and in China as well as in Palestine and Mesopotamia. It is to this exceptional conjunction of a changing male outlook in the ancient agricultural societies and an irresistible tidal wave of nomadic patriarchal invaders that history owes this global revolution."

Individual men could have heard about the new biology as they travelled and traded, or when strangers came into their lands. But however they heard about the male-seed idea, and if they believed it, their reaction would have been one of shock. They suddenly realised they didn't know their roots. All the time they'd been tracing their ancestry through their mother's line, they should've been tracing it through their father. And many men would not have known who their father was – a loss they must have felt deeply. No doubt there were many men who felt cheated, and angry.

This was a unique revolution in that it polarised men and women in a powerful way – either she was the source of life, or he was. Nobody could prove their case. People could 'agree to differ' and come to an answer that gave a kind of equality. There had been versions of that over time – especially the red/white theories: she contributes the red parts of the baby; he contributes the white. The problem with that was people gave relative value to the red or white, usually saying the white was superior because it contributed the bones, eyes and brain. And, also, there were those who stood back from the whole question and said reproduction was the will of god, or the goddess, and that was another argument.

How long it took for the patriarchal idea to take hold in a particular area depended on many things. Places that were hard to reach, especially the islands in the Mediterranean Sea, maintained the female-centred view longer. People living in places where there was a cataclysmic event leading to crop failure – a natural disaster or climate change – may have been more inclined to disown the old goddesses and adopt the new gods. Another factor was invasion by a patriarchal force.

Although, on a global scale, the male-seed revolution took a few thousand years to accomplish, on a local level the conversion may have been swift. Small communities could be dealt with by killing all the men and male children – which gets rid of the enemy's seed. By also killing the older women, the old female-centred ideas die with them. That left the younger women and girls who the patriarchal invaders could use as baby-making machines.

In other places, where the numbers of people were too many to allow such drastic measures, the invaders had to bide their time, promote their 'new biology,' and take over the power-base shrine by shrine – all the while watching the old women die and with them, knowledge of the old ways. There would always be local men for whom the new biology made perfect sense, and who were willing to accept the new gods, and rule on the invader's behalf. Despite the horror of forcible invasions, for men there was the compensation that came with the new biology – the children now 'belonged' to them.

By 2,100 BC in the Sumerian city of Ur, the patriarchal control of women was already in full swing. In the Laws of Ur-Namma (6) it states that "if a man violates the right of another and deflowers the virgin wife of a young man, they shall kill that male" – men now appear to have rights over women. In law (7), if a wife initiates sex with another "they shall kill that woman; that man shall be released" – female adultery is heavily punished. The same was the case in the kingdom of Eshnunna (law 28) around 1,770 BC: "the day she is seized in the lap of another man, she shall die, she will not live."

In the city of Assur, around 1,076 BC, the Middle Assyrian law (A/40) stated that wives, widows, and daughters should be veiled in the street. But a prostitute who goes veiled gets 50 blows with rods and hot pitch over her head. Veiling came into being because during wars the enemy men were killed and the women captured, so many were made to prostitute themselves on the street. Veiling was used to distinguish these women, and other slave women, from female citizens including concubines.

We can see that the patriarchal attitude was established in Sumeria by 2,000 BC. Yet throughout the wider region people were still continuing practices from much earlier times and resisting change, and would continue to do so for many centuries to come. This was an 'all or nothing' battle of the sexes, far more extreme than anything we experience today. In the previous sections we saw that the blood-line began with ancestry being reckoned along the female line, societies were matrilineal, spiritual authority was held by women, and developed into queenship, women were the heads of households, had authority within society, and sexual freedom.

None of these things would be tolerated when men gained confidence in the idea that they were the only source of human seed and felt the need to control the means of their reproduction – women.

SELECTED REFERENCES:
Riencourt, de, Amaury, *Women and Power in History*, London: Honeyglen Publishing Ltd., 1983, pages 34-35.
Roth, Martha T, *Law Collections from Mesopotamia and Asia Minor*, Atlanta: Scholar's Press, 1995, pages in order 17, 18, 63, and 68.

58: NATIVE AMERICANS: A TAKE-OVER AND COVER-UP

The decimation of Native American life and culture began around 1,500 AD with the invasion of Spanish Christians. They were shocked to find people paying homage to a female creative spirit, and a society in which women were owners of the land, and central to the power structure of society.

In *The Sacred Hoop*, former Professor of American Indian Studies at the University of California, Paula Gunn Allen, writes about "hundreds of tribes forced into patriarchal modes" and of female-run tribes of which little written evidence exists, including the Montagnais-Naskapi, Navajo, Crow, Hopi, Pomo, Turok, Kiowa and Natchez in North America, and the Bari and Mapiche in South America "to name just a few." (DNA evidence for an elite matriline in Chaco Canyon, NM, between 800-1,130 AD was published in 2017). Allen grew up in the Keres tribe, with the oral tradition still around her, and made it her life's work to record Native American memories and legends before they faded into final obscurity. She found the female Creative Spirit described as the 'power of intelligence,' the 'Old Woman who tends the fires of life' and, as Old Spider Woman, the one who 'weaves us together in a fabric of interconnection':

"There is a spirit that pervades everything, that is capable of powerful song and radiant movement, and that moves in and out of the mind. The colours of this spirit are multitudinous, a glowing, pulsing rainbow. Old Spider Woman is one name for this quintessential spirit, and Serpent Woman is another. Corn Woman is one aspect of her, and

Earth Woman is another, and what they together have made is called Creation, Earth, creatures, plants and light."

The great female spirit is in the very last stages of being lost, and replaced by male counterparts, including the generic 'Great Spirit':

"The Hopi goddess Spider Woman has become the masculine Maseo or Tawa, referred to in the masculine, and the Zuni goddess is on her way to malehood. Changing Woman of the Navajo has contenders for her position, while the Keres Thought Woman trembles on the brink of displacement by her sister-goddess-cum-god Utset. Among the Cherokee, the goddess of the river foam is easily replaced by Thunder in many tales, and the Iroquois divinity Sky Woman now gets her ideas and powers from her dead father or her monstrous grandson."

The process of take-over took many centuries, and many forms. By the early nineteenth century, the clan-mother rule had been changed by the Code of Handsome Lake, to the classic rule of the nuclear family patriarch. And when early academics – male, of course – looked at Native American cultures they applied the usual patriarchal perspective, and in doing so almost 'disappeared' what was left of the female traditions:

"Women's rituals, ceremonies, traditions, customs, attitudes, values, activities, philosophies, ceremonial and social positions, histories, medicine societies, and shamanistic identities – that is, all the oral tradition that is in every sense and on every level the literature of the tribe – have been largely ignored by folklorists, ethnographers, and literary critics in the field of American Indian studies. These traditions have never been described or examined in terms of their proper, that is, woman-focused, context. Actually, it is primarily the context that has been ignored – vanished, disappeared, buried under tons of scholarly materials selected and erected to hide the centrality of women in tribal society, tribal literature, and tribal hearts and minds."

Allen describes how the Iroquois federal system was made up of local, then 'state,' then 'federal' bodies, each of which had executive, legislative, and judicial branches. Spiritual understanding underpinned policy at all levels and because The Council of Matrons were the ceremonial centre of the system, general policy was decided by them. Matters of justice were decided by men and women together, but The Council of Matrons had a say in which men could join in that decision-making process. Once in The Council, a Matron could not be dis-empowered unless she herself violated certain laws, one of which was that, if she married, she should not take her husband's name.

Women were central in the power structure because they were credited with having the primary potency – transformative power:

"The old ones were empowered by their certain knowledge that the power to make life is the source and model for all ritual magic and that no other power can gainsay it. Nor is that power really biological at base; it is the power of ritual magic, the power of Thought, of Mind, that gives rise to biological organisms as it gives rise to social organisations, material culture, and transformations of all kinds – including hunting, war, healing, spirit communication, rain-making and all the rest."

We're very lucky that the Native American oral tradition could still be heard in the mid-20th century. It's taken five hundred years, since the first invaders, for the female-centred traditions to nearly disappear. If the patriarchal take-over had happened a hundred years earlier, they'd probably be nothing left of the female traditions to grab back from the misty sound waves of time. Now imagine how easy it's been for men to disappear female-centred cultures that existed not hundreds but thousands of years ago.

SELECTED REFERENCES:
Allen, Paula Gunn, *The Sacred Hoop*, 1986, quotes from pages, in order: 13, 41, 268 and 28. Copyright © 1986, 1992 by Paula Gunn Allen. Reprinted by permission of Beacon Press, Boston.
Kennett, Douglas J., et al, Archaeogenomic evidence reveals prehistoric matrilineal dynasty, Nature Communications 8, Article number 14115 (2017).

59: YAHWEH: ANOTHER TAKE-OVER

The Israelites developed from a diverse group of animal-herding immigrants from outside Canaan, probably extended family and clans, joining with people from within Canaan. They migrated and settled in the sparsely populated hill country, some distance from the long-settled coastal cities and farming lowlands. The word 'Canaan' means 'Land of Purple' because the Canaanites extracted purple dye from a local shellfish. Their coastal cities included Ashkelon and, far to the north, Ugarit, which had a defensive wall as early as 6,000 BC. The time we know most about though is between 1,500 and 1,200 BC, when Ugarit was the centre of Canaanite high culture. Many cuneiform clay tablets have been unearthed by archaeologists and although the huge site is still being excavated ninety years after its discovery, we know Ugarit had at least four libraries and a palace with ninety rooms. Canaan was a sophisticated international trading community.

One temple found at Ugarit was dedicated to Dagon, god of grain and agriculture, said to have invented the plough. This tells us that in Biblical times people were leaving behind the idea of a female source of seed, and thinking in terms of a male one. Ugarit also had a temple to Ba'al, god of rain, thunder and fertility. But the chief of the gods was El, and his wife/consort was Asherah.

Over the millennia, and in various places around the ancient Near East, this goddess was known by several names including Astarte, Ashtart, and in the Bible her name was conflated with the Phoenician goddess Ashtoreth. Originally, Astarte and another Ugarit goddesses, Anat, were worshipped as deities in their own rights, without a husband or partner. But by the time the Israelite story begins, her name was Asherah and she was the consort of El. Their son, Ba'al, was extremely important to the farming Canaanites because he brought rain. His voice was said to be in the clouds, a beautiful description of thunder, and he would flash his lightening to earth.

The Israelites and Canaanites lived side by side for hundreds of years, speaking the same language, and the Israelites used Canaanite shrines and adopted their traditions and religious practices. Because the Israelites didn't yet have an established culture of their own, they also adopted the artistic culture of the Canaanites, including their style of poetry, and they used administration techniques learnt from the Egyptians.

The Israelites were drawn to the Canaanite pantheon of gods, not only because that helped integrate them with their new-found neighbours, but because when they started farming, they needed rain too. The Israelite god, YHWH, or Yahweh, was a god of war more appropriate for nomads, and not very helpful to the Canaanites, who already had El as their chief god. So, to promote the singular god, Yahweh, the Israelite priests had to overcome El, Asherah, and Ba'al. All three needed taking down, and the battle would be fought in several steps.

The first to be dealt with was El. Step one involved appropriating his name, so in various ways we see the name 'El' linked with Yahweh, such as Beth-el (Genesis 31:13) and El-beth-el (Gen. 35:7). Even the name 'Israel,' which in Hebrew is yisra'el, means 'El rules' or, some say, 'the champions of God.'

Next, the wife of El was appropriated so she could be seen as the wife of Yahweh. We've archaeological evidence from the early Israelite period in the form of inscriptions and illustrations linking Asherah with Yahweh, making them the divine couple. Asherah was strongly associated with serpents, and both she and they represented fertility. Asherah was readily accepted as the goddess of Israel, and became an integral part of the official religion. She was represented in many forms – as a female image, a green tree, a tree trunk, or a wooden pole known as an asherim, and worshipped in groves of trees, often on a hill.

The Israelite religion promoted the idea of one god, not many gods who divided the work between them, with one in charge of rain, another in charge of the earth, or sun, or sky, and so forth. But the Canaanites liked having their different gods, especially Asherah, who they'd worshipped for millennia in one form or another, and Ba'al, who brought rain, crops, and food.

The Israelite religion also involved a covenant between the people and Yahweh, which made the people responsible for events such as weather and invasions/war: if they behaved themselves, Yahweh would look kindly upon them and all would go well; if they didn't behave, there would be trouble. The Canaanite religion didn't have the same sense of personal responsibility because things like rain were dependent on gods like Ba'al, and all they had to do to ensure the rain fell was provide offerings, and carry out the traditional rituals.

One of these was the annual 'sacred marriage' (*hieros gamos*), which was a public display of sex between male farmers and female temple prostitutes, meant to represent the sexual union of god and goddess. This was a type of sympathetic marriage – the idea being that because men and women do what's necessary to reproduce, the rains would fall, irrigate the earth, and bring fruition to the crops as well. This display didn't go down well with the Israelite priests who were outraged by the sexual licentiousness of the people, especially the women. Promiscuous sex isn't a problem for people who reckon descent through the female, but it is reproductive anarchy for those who reckon descent through the male.

Nevertheless, at the beginning of their time in Canaan the Israelites did worship the goddess and make offerings to her at official cult sanctuaries and altars, officiated at by cult personnel. Her symbols were very much a part of Israelite life, to the extent that King David's own son, Rehoboam, erected an asherim in Jerusalem, where it remained until the 8th Century BC, when the reforming Hezekiah destroyed it. She was known as 'the queen of heaven,' 'the mother of all deities,' 'celestial ruler' and 'the mistress of kingship.' From the time of the Canaanite occupation, the late Bronze Age, archaeologists have found upright female figures representing Asherah and displaying symbols of her divinity. Then, in the early Iron Age, around the time the Israelites were ruled by the 'Judges,' we begin to see many examples of flat, oval-shaped, plaques – the 'graven' images so often referred to in The Bible. These were mass produced from moulds in pottery and showed the naked goddess Asherah with her arms raised, holding serpents or the stalks of lilies in her hands. This is when things began to change and the people were forbidden to worship the goddess any longer.

The plaques were flat for a reason. We hear time and time again in the Bible that the 'children of Israel' forsook the Lord, and served Ba'al and Ashtaroth – which refers to multiple idols of the goddess (Judges 2:13). The reluctance of the people to adhere to the new religion of Yahweh was a constant source of aggravation to the Levite and Aaronite priests and necessitated the introduction of a spirit police, as Rabbi Louis Ginzberg tells us with this story about King Josiah:

"The efforts of the king on behalf of God and His law found no echo with the great majority of the people. Though the king was successful in preventing the worship of idols in public, his subjects knew how to deceive him. Josiah sent out his pious sympathisers to inspect the houses of the people, and he was satisfied with their report, that they had found no idols, not suspecting that the recreant people had fastened half an image on each wing of the doors, so that the inmates faced their household idols as they closed the door upon Josiah's inspectors."

The prophets Jeremiah, Ezra, Nehemiah and Hosea spent most of their time trying to stamp out idolatry. In Jeremiah 44:16-18 we hear how he went to Egypt to try and convince the Jews living there to stop their evil-doing and threatened them, on behalf of the God Yahweh, with punishment "by the sword, by the famine and by the pestilence." The crowd at Pathros were not impressed. They replied:

"... we will not hearken unto thee. But we will certainly do whatsoever thing goeth forth out of our own mouth, to burn incense unto the queen of heaven, and to pour out drink offerings unto her, as we have done, we, and our fathers, our kings, and our princes, in the cities of Judah, and in the streets of Jerusalem: for then we had plenty of victuals, and were well, and saw no evil. But since we left off to burn incense to the queen of heaven, and to pour our drink offerings unto her, we have wanted all things, and have been consumed by the sword and by the famine."

Yahweh reacted with vengeance:

"I will watch over them for evil, and not for good: and all the men of Judah that are in the land of Egypt shall be consumed by the sword and by the famine, until there be an end of them." (Jer. 44:27)

This was written around 580 BC, and shows that the Israelites were still determined to worship 'the queen of heaven' almost a thousand years after Moses had told them this:

"Ye shall utterly destroy all the places, wherein the nations which ye shall possess served their gods, upon the high mountains, and upon the hills, and under every green tree:
And ye shall overthrow their altars, and break their pillars, and burn their groves with fire; and ye shall hew down the graven images of their gods and destroy the names of them out of that place." (Deuteronomy 12:2-3)

So hateful was the worship of other gods, it apparently warranted murdering your own child:

"If your brother or son or daughter or wife or friend suggest serving other gods, you must kill him, your hand must be the first raised in putting him to death and all the people shall follow you." (Deuteronomy 13:6)

Despite all these harsh words, the people still followed the old gods and goddesses, and the Old Testament records the struggle between the good, the followers of Yahweh, and the bad, the idolaters. Gideon was good because he built an altar to

Yahweh and followed his instructions to "pull down the altar of Ba'al which belongs to your father, and cut down the Asherah that is beside it" (Judges 6:25). Queen Maachah was dethroned by her son Asa because she was bad and "made an idol in a grove" (1 Kings 15:13). These dramas were played out century after century as the old ways were replaced by the new.

The Israelite priests used every tool at their disposal to try and eradicate the old gods and goddesses. There was threat of, and actual, physical violence. The people were encouraged to tear down false altars, and were sent into their neighbours' homes to look for idols to destroy. Supposedly the false religion was eradicated by Jehu (2 Kings 10:26-28) but it was still felt enough of a threat that, when the story of the Israelites came to be written in the Bible, the details were changed somewhat.

Although the ancient texts and artefacts show that Yahweh and Asherah were worshipped as the divine couple, in the Bible this aspect of history has been completely airbrushed out. The 'disappearance' of the divine female happened in several ways. Asherah is simply ignored, and referred to as a tree or grove of trees and the whole concept of a female goddess is side-stepped. Also, she's linked with Ba'al in a way that's not confirmed in ancient texts, even from Canaanite Ugarit. Ba'al was major opposition to the religion of Yahweh and he was portrayed as diabolical so linking Asherah with him discredited her, and those who worshipped her. Her name was changed so it incorporated letters from the Hebrew word for 'shame' – boshet, and we see her for the first time called Ashtoret – woman of shame. And the serpent with which she'd so long been associated became the epitome of evil. Good had become bad, and the take-over was complete.

Or perhaps not so complete. The Orthodox tradition considers a person to be Jewish only if their mother is Jewish. Yet, in all other ways, inheritance and descent is reckoned along the male line. Jewish monarchy followed the male line. The twelve tribes of Israel started with Jacob's twelve sons: Reuben,

Simeon, Levi, Judah, Issachar, Zebulun, Dan, Naphtali, Manasseh, Ephraim, Benjamin, Gad, Asher. Each of these tribes is then subdivided by the number of sons their male tribal ancestor had. These families are again subdivided according to the male sons, and so forth. This is clearly a male line of identity, with each individual being a member of the same 'house' as their father. In the case of a marriage between a man and woman from different 'houses,' their children gain their identity from the father's 'house,' or line. Judaism is a patrilineal culture – so what is the reason for the importance of the Jewish mother?

Some say it started in the 4th century BC with Ezra, others that it was during Roman rule, probably at the centre of Rabbinical learning in Yavneh in the 1st century AD. However, The Talmud – in which Judaism's Oral Law was recorded in the 2nd century, indicates it had always been the case that a person was Jewish because their mother was Jewish. This raises an interesting point. In classical Judaism there are, in addition to the three patriarchs of Abraham, Isaac and Jacob, four 'mothers': the two wives of Jacob, Leah and Rachel; Jacob's mother, Rebekah; and Jacob's grandmother, Sarah – the wife of Abraham. This 3-generation family are where the Hebrew tribes began. Sarah was born in 1,986 BC at a time when 'beena marriage' was the norm – with the man moving on marriage to the wife's tent and clan. Matriarchal traditions may well have been the norm at this time. As we know, the Hebrew people had to be persuaded to give up 'the queen of heaven,' and refused even when they were threatened with death. Their reluctance to accept the new order was a source of consternation to the priests for well over a thousand years. So here's my question – did the Hebrew people insist on keeping their traditional mother-right even as they accepted the patrilineal line of inheritance? Do we see here another example of how the old ways become incorporated into the new?

SELECTED REFERENCES:

Ginzberg, Louis, page 616. Reprinted from *Legends of The Bible*, © 1956, Louis Ginzberg, published by The Jewish Publication Society, Philadelphia, with permission of the publisher.

60: ADAM AND EVE

The Biblical story of Adam and Eve was a take-over of an earlier Sumerian myth, rewritten for the patriarchal age. Both say the garden is bordered by four rivers, and both have forbidden fruit. In the Sumerian version, the minor male god Enki disobeys the higher female divine order, the Mother-Goddess. Enki was in transition from waterer to inseminator and his disobedience and challenge to the goddess would have been well understood by the people at the time. Gerda Lerner gives more detail:

"The description of the Garden of Eden parallels the Sumerian garden of creation, which is also described as a place bordered by four great rivers. In the Sumerian creation myth, Mother-Goddess Ninhursag allowed eight lovely plants to sprout in the garden, but the gods were forbidden to eat from them. Still, the water-god Enki ate from them, and Ninhursag condemned him to die. Accordingly, eight of Enki's organs fell ill. The fox appealed on his behalf, and the Goddess agreed to commute sentence of death. She created a special healing deity for each afflicted organ. When it came to the rib, she said: 'To the goddess Ninti I have given birth for you.' In Sumerian the word 'Ninti' has a double meaning, namely, 'female ruler of the rib' and 'female ruler of life'."

The Sumerian word 'Ninti' is a combination of the word for female ruler 'Nin' (as in Nin-hursag), and '*ti*,' which can translate as both 'rib' and 'to make live.' So, while in the Sumerian version a play of words gives special significance to the rib in the recovery of Enki, in the Biblical version the birth of Eve is located in the rib. By the time Genesis came to be written there was one thing paramount in men's minds – female chastity – and that is why the rib was chosen, according to Rabbi Louis Ginzberg in *Legends of the Bible*:

"When God was on the point of making Eve, He said: 'I will not make her from the head of man, lest she carry her head high in arrogant pride; not from the eye, lest she be wanton-eyed: not from the ear, lest she be an eavesdropper; not from the neck, lest she be insolent; not from the mouth, lest she be a tattler; not from the heart, lest she be a meddler; not from the foot, lest she be a gadabout. I will form her from a chaste portion of the body, and to every limb and organ as He formed it, God said 'Be chaste! Be chaste!' Nevertheless, in spite of the great caution used, woman has all the faults God tried to obviate."

The serpent in the Adam and Eve story is a direct representation of the goddess. From earliest times, images of goddesses were literally entwined with snakes. The snake or serpent was associated with the goddesses Ua Zit, Hathor, Nidaba, Ninlil, Inanna, later Ishtar, Tiamat, Athena, Hera, Gaia and others. The goddess and snake appeared together in Canaan, Egypt, Crete, Cyprus, Babylon, and elsewhere. It was, therefore, inevitable that the serpent should be chosen as the creature which enticed Eve into disobeying the word of God and causing humanity's banishment from the Garden of Eden, and the start of all our woes.

Ginzberg tells us that the serpent's poison was "the poison of evil inclination" and that after the serpent had plucked the fruit for Eve she "opened the gate of Paradise and he slipped in." The euphemism for sexual intercourse is easy enough to draw, given the phallic shape of the serpent and the unashamed sexuality of goddess worship.

The serpent hid in a tree sometimes referred to as 'the tree of knowledge' and at other times, 'the tree of life.' They're one and the same thing because the knowledge was about life itself – where we come from. No knowledge is more important. And if you think of the tree of life as holding knowledge about good and evil, it's still the same subject because the most evil thing –

to the patriarchs – was following in the ways of the goddess, being sexually promiscuous, and confusing the big issue – who is the father?

Not only did the Adam and Eve story illustrate to women that they were foolish if they followed in the ways of the goddess, it also gave men a weapon to keep women barred from positions of authority, especially with regard to spiritual matters. Christian churches codify the laws governing their affairs in the *Code of Canon Law* and the first comprehensive version was put together in the 12th century by an Italian lawyer called Gratian. It became the textbook on church law until 1917, and influenced the secular world as well. Because of Eve, women's place was to be under men's direction:

"Woman's authority is nil; let her in all things be subject to the rule of man ... And neither can she teach nor be a witness, nor give a guarantee, nor sit in judgement. Adam was beguiled by Eve, not she by him. It is right that he whom woman led into wrongdoing should have her under his direction, so that he may not fail a second time through female levity."

When God made Adam He "breathed into his nostrils the breath of life; and man became a living soul" (Genesis Ch. 2:7). But Eve wasn't given "a living soul." This distinction is not accidental. Only men passed "the breath of life" through their seed to the next generation. Women had no seed so they were an evolutionary dead-end. The 13th century philosopher and theologian, Thomas Aquinas, talked about this distinction in his work *Summa Theologica*, which influenced European thought for centuries. He refers to the second place in Genesis where God created "male and female" (Ch. 5:1-2), saying "in a secondary sense the image of God is found in man, and not in woman: for man is the beginning and end of woman; as God is the beginning and end of every creature." He thought that woman comes from male seed, and she's an imperfect being:

"As regards the individual nature, woman is defective and misbegotten, for the active force in the male seed tends to the production of a perfect likeness in the masculine sex; while the production of woman comes from a defect in the active force or from some material indisposition, or even from some external influence..."

Misogyny is the hatred of women and it festered where two ideas met. The first idea is that women can't be trusted – a notion greatly amplified by the story of Adam and Eve. Trust is important to men because while a woman can be certain a child is hers, a man cannot. Men fear that women will have sex with another man, and they won't know whose child she has. The second idea was that women are inferior because they weren't given the precious seed of life. Of course that was a mistake, as we know. However, it led to the notion that women are reproductive helpmates and, because they have no seed, have no reproductive rights themselves. This idea gave men an inflated sense of their own importance, and downgraded women. Men's sense of reproductive superiority and the disrespect of women this engendered, in conjunction with men's fear of women, proved a lethal combination for women.

SELECTED REFERENCES:
Lerner, Gerda, *The Creation of Patriarchy*, Oxford: Oxford University Press, 1986, pages 184-5. By permission of Oxford University Press Inc. www.oup.com.
Ginzberg, Louis, page 35. Reprinted from *Legends of The Bible*, © 1956, Louis Ginzberg, published by The Jewish Publication Society, Philadelphia, with permission of the publisher.
Gratian, *Decretum*, Italy, 12th century.

61: LIVING A DOUBLE LIFE

There have been three major shifts in thinking about reproduction:

FROM	TO
1. Women reproduce on their own.	Women have the seed within them.
2. Women have the seed within them.	Men have the seed within them.
3. Men have the seed within them.	Both men and women have the seed within them.

Shift 2) occurred in early Israelite history and took over a thousand years. People resisted. And here's the thing: reproduction theories are just that – theories. Nobody can prove anything. At least they couldn't until shift 3) – and even that took 133 years from start to finish, scientifically speaking.

Some people live with one idea their whole lives. They know nothing else. But many people live with two ideas side by side. When the anthropologist Malinowski landed on the Trobriand Islands in 1914 he found that having promiscuous sex was not only the norm, but that the most promiscuous girl was the most admired. He was shocked. The missionaries soon arrived to convert the naughty heathens. They built a church, which the Trobrianders still happily go to, but then they just get on with their lives in the way they always have.

Another culture that's living a double life are the Minangkabau of Sumatra in Indonesia. As Muslims, they pray five times a day and observe the other practices of Islam yet, according to Richard Mahler, "they see no conflict with their Minangkabau customs," which are matrilineal:

"... within the family, the eldest woman is responsible for all important decisions affecting the group, although she may often consult with other female family members before making those decisions."

The Minangkabau value girls more than boys:

"The birth of a daughter is cause for celebration, and a pair of sharp peaks is added to the steeply pitched roof to signal the blessed event. In

fact, travellers can determine the number of girls in a family by counting the points on a Minangkabau house and dividing by two."

Islam only arrived in Indonesia in the sixteenth century, and probably reached the Minangkabau some time after that, but their own culture is thousands of years older. Interestingly, the back-and-forth nature of the matriarchy-patriarchy changes has been recorded by Nancy Tanner who says that during the Dutch colonial period the nature of the matrilineal customs changed so that the mother's brothers became controlling. But 80 or so years later, there's a much greater degree of female autonomy as the people have returned to the traditional ways, with the mothers themselves in control. You'd think, perhaps, that once men had tasted power, they'd never allow a return to the female-centred ways but this isn't so, as Richard Mahler found out:

"In my conversations with Miningkabau men, they seemed to be relatively content with the situation and often turned over all their income to their wives, who gave them a small allowance or pocket money ... Several men told me that when they were young they went off to live on Java or Bali to get out from under the presumed yoke of female dominance, only to return to the Minangkabau area because they found they preferred their original way of life after all."

It's possible there were many places where the old female-centred cultures lingered, long after patriarchal overlords or religions officially took over the land. And there have no doubt been many places where there was a back-and-forth battle. To an outsider, these cultural changes might appear confusing and paradoxical. But to the person actually living with conflicting life-views, it may seem quite normal. What is clear is that 'official' religions don't necessarily affect traditional customs, and invading armies don't always exert a deep influence on the traditional ways of the people they have under their military control.

Revolutions come in many forms. In some places they may be swift and complete. In others, a long period of time is involved and, looking from the outside, the culture seems complex as it doesn't fit with the stereotypes of 'matriarchal' or 'patriarchal.' But this is the nature of transition, and we need to get used to it – especially when writing history, or digging up the past.

As a reminder of how complex transitions can be, we only need to look at ourselves. The male-seed idea of reproduction fell into scientific disrepute around the turn of the 20th century. There was a cover-up, so very few people know the names of the scientists responsible for that revolution in reproduction theory. But, from then on, the new science was taught, so men who'd previously been able to say that women are 'naturally' inferior, no longer had ground to stand on. Pretty soon we had women marching in the street and demanding the vote, as well as other rights denied to them. In the 1960's things really took off in terms of 'women's liberation,' and from then it was a straight road to where we are today. And where are we? We're in our own transitional phase, from patriarchy to equality.

Around the world today women are in different places with regard to their liberation journey. Some are only beginning, and feeling the full force of the patriarchal backlash. But the theory that underpinned patriarchal logic has gone, even if the traditions haven't. Each woman will have to evaluate her cultural situation and make her own choice as to how fast and how far she wishes to go. And we all need to support each other in the choices we make. But one thing is certain: change will come to us all – sooner or later.

SELECTED REFERENCES:
Mahler, Richard, *Matriarchy Research and Reclaim Network Newsletter*, No 74, Autumn 1991, page 21.
Tanner, Nancy, 'Minangkabau,' in LeBar, Frank (Ed.), *Insular Southeast Asia: Ethnographic Studies, Section 7, Sumatra – Vol.1*, New Haven: Human Relations Area Files (HRAF) Press, 1976, pages 1-82.

PART FIVE

62: "I THOUGHT PEOPLE HAVE ALWAYS KNOWN THE FACTS OF LIFE"

Here's the crazy thing: although every single person born asks the question "where did I come from?" that important subject – reproduction theory – is not discussed academically at all. It plays no part in feminist theory, theology, philosophy, history or archaeology. Apparently, all the specialists in these fields seem to think "people have always known the facts of life." I accuse them of dereliction of duty because it is simply impossible to understand any of those subjects without recognising that people had the facts of life wrong.

And, without considering reproduction theory, it is impossible to understand the profound differences today between cultures with regard to their views about the position of women in society. Different cultures look at each other across a huge and profound chasm of misunderstanding. And this can lead to conflict.

The facts of life were incredibly hard to establish. Imagine how difficult it must have been without a microscope. All you know is what you see. Plant seeds are singular; butterflies emerge fully formed from their chrysalis; maggots crawl out of rotten meat. These natural events of creation, and many others, were argued about for millennia. When it came to human reproduction people weren't working with facts, only clues – and those clues sent them down one wrong track after the other.

I don't care about the past. What happened in the 5th century AD, or the 5th millennium BC, didn't affect me. I wasn't there. I'm here now, and I care about the women and children living in cultures rooted in the tradition that males are 'naturally' superior. That includes women beaten by men to 'keep them in their place,' and female babies who'll be murdered today, and tomorrow, and every day this week, because they're thought to be an evolutionary dead-end. Female infanticide is an outcome of societies thinking it's a waste of money to bring up a daughter who will be 'given away' to provide children for another family – her husband's.

Patriarchal traditions envelop women like a shroud. Some of us can fight our way out, but millions of women around the world are stuck in that confining apparel from birth to death. And they're so used to it, they've no idea what personal freedom means.

People living in past historical times were ignorant, and it's pointless holding to their rules and regulations. They were living with a huge mistake – it was understandable, even logical, but it was wrong. So to hark back to those days as if they understood some fundamental truth about the essential 'nature' of men and women is ridiculous.

It's actually very dangerous to look back at old scripture and read it as timeless wisdom. It was written by people who were very afraid of losing everything – their parentage, their children, and their land. The Bible says if you discover people "serve other gods" (Deuteronomy 13:13):

"Thou shalt surely smite the inhabitants of that city with the edge of the sword, destroying it utterly, and all that is therein, and the cattle thereof, with the edge of the sword." (Deuteronomy 13:15)

The hatefulness in this passage only begins to make sense when we understand the part reproduction theory played in people's lives. It is not about worshipping "other gods" – a pantheon of miscellaneous gods, rather than the one, true God. It's about a male-seed monotheistic religion fighting a battle with the old goddess religions. This was not simply a spiritual question. The old female-centred religions denied men parentage in a genetic/seed sense. They reckoned descent through the female – from mother back in time to her mother and so on; there was no male parentage as such. So a man stood to lose his own father, lose being a father to his children, lose authority, and land. There was a colossal clash of reproductive ignorance and this was what the battles in the Old Testament were about.

All three monotheistic religions of Judaism, Christianity, and Islam, trace their heritage back to Abraham. His father, known as Terah in the Bible and as Azar in the Qu'ran, was an idolater. Not only did he worship idols, he carved and sold them in his shop. Terah was born around 2,056 BC, and idolatry was then the way of life. In the Qu'ran, Sura 6:79, Abraham says, "I disown your idols. I will turn my face to Him who has created the heavens and the earth, and will live a righteous life. I am no idolater." Abraham burnt his father's shop and started the practice of worshipping one male God. But from this time on, battles would be fought with idolaters for thousands of years. As late as the 7th century, at the time of the Prophet Mohammed, people were worshipping the goddesses Al-Lat, Al-Uzza, and Manat even though, as it says in Sura 53:23, "the guidance of their Lord has long since come to them."

It took over two and a half thousand years, from Abraham to Mohammed, to bring idolatry to an end, and in that long time the meaning of idol worship changed. At the beginning, Abraham was battling a culture that would not give up the idea of female seed, and reckoned ancestry through the female. By Mohammed's time, the male seed idea of reproduction was fully established and worship of females was probably about them being intermediaries – figures who would speak to God on behalf of the worshipper.

When researchers look at ancient artefacts and translate ancient documents they need to try and answer this question "where did they think babies come from?" Up to now, they've been blind to this crucial subject, and lazily reached for the word "fertility" as if it meant something. Right now, reproduction theory is a non-subject that needs to become a fully formed subject and included in all relevant fields of study.

Vis-à-vis reproduction, humanity is in a very dangerous

position because we have an odd combination of ignorance and knowledge existing side by side. There are people in the world today who still don't know the facts of life, and those who carry on with traditions built on a profound mistake that was both logical and inevitable, but wrong all the same. Because they are looking to the past, they can't fully embrace the future. At the same time, there's an extraordinary level of knowledge regarding the building blocks of life, and DNA is no longer locked into cells. 'Synthetic biology' is the new hobby in which amateur enthusiasts can buy DNA on the internet and experiment with making new life. Geneticists recognise the danger posed by their field and meet up at international conferences to try and decide what they should do with their new power. They discuss CRISPER-Cas 9 and gene drive, which together can bring about the complete rewriting of the germ line. It's official – we can play God. At present, goats are bred with spider genes so their milk can be spun into very strong, fine fibres, mosquitoes are bred to be sterile, and salmon are bred with other fish species to speed up their rate of growth and size. This is just the beginning. But in the future plants, insects, fish, birds, animals, and people, will all be genetically manipulated in ways we cannot now imagine, and may be unable to control.

The profound scientific changes now taking place will affect every person living on the planet. Are we ready for that future? Men took control of the past and still have control today and judging from the history of war around the world, and the critical state of the planet, collectively they did not do a great job. Their legacy includes the fact that every single day 17,000 children under five will die, half of them from starvation. This daily genocide is largely preventable but governments don't have the will to deal with it. They're too busy manufacturing armaments and fighting wars.

Men have been indulged to such a degree, and given so much control, they are now completely out of control. Maybe I watch too much news, but I don't believe that if women had equal control all this diabolical behaviour would be allowed to continue. Men need reigning in, and they need to get over the notion that they have some natural, traditional, right to run the world. Yes, they did run the world, but they were only allowed to do it because we were all ignorant about their relative value and entitlement. Men need to realise that those days have gone.

Women too need to step into the future and stop lingering in the past. Just leave it behind. We have the choice to walk away from violent, or sexist, or lazy men. Being angry about men's behaviour in the past and in the present doesn't help us. We could take inspiration from the ancient Greek play Lysistrata, written in 411 BC, in which women denied men sex until they stopped the Peloponnesian war. We've had 5,000 years of patriarchy during which men butchered each other, women, and children, lorded it over their wives, and enjoyed their elevated position while women cleaned up after them. Now they need to join the 21st century. A bird does not fly on one wing; it takes two wings to fly. Men and women are equal, and if we can learn to fly we might just be able to save ourselves and the planet. And one thing is for sure – we'd all have a better time.

Made in the USA
Columbia, SC
30 May 2017